The
Bull
Didn't Win

*What One Family Learned
About Faith After a TBI*

JACOB BROWDER
& SUSAN BROWDER

Foreword

Susan and Jacob Browder wrote their book, "The Bull Didn't Win," from both of their perspectives. You will get to know the mom, Susan, as she lets you see her son's injury and recovery through her eyes. You will learn so much about Jacob, the young man who suffered a traumatic brain injury at a bull riding school, as he takes you on the toughest ride of his life. This mom and son will leave you with an inspiring story that will motivate you to get through the hardest of times. Parts of the book are only told by Susan as Jacob is in a coma fighting for his life.

Praise for *The Bull Didn't Win*

"That is all a father wants for his son—to live a life pursuing his dreams."

—Nicky Browder

"Challenges and pain can push you, but your dreams can pull you a lot faster! The bull Didn't Win, Jacob did! This is why we remind others often that it's not about what we go through it's about what we GROW through- Which is why I like to say we don't need it to be easy we just need it to be possible!"

—Timothy Alexander

"To witness the courage, confidence and concerned faith of a Momma like this is rare in today's age. Deep calls to deep and the invitation to go is very present. From the ashes he makes beautiful things and you get the sense that we are only getting to see the beginning of the Harvest here. I'm already excited for whatever is next."

—LeAnn Hart

The
Bull
Didn't Win

JACOB AND
SUSAN BROWDER

Published by P e r s o n a   P u b l i s h i n g
A wholly owned subsidary of Story Launcher LLC,
50 Fifteen Mile Trail. Meeteetse, Wyo 82433
www.StoryLauncher.com

The Bull Didn't Win

Cover image: Evelyn McCarter
photography@gmail.com
Book cover design by www.digitalcc.us
Book interior design www.digitalcc.us
Editing by Story Launcher's Greta Baranowski

Author's books are available for order through Amazon.com

LinkedIn: linkedin.com/in/susan-browder-thebulldidntwin
Twitter: @swbrowder
Instagram: @jacob_browder @susanbrowder
Facebook: https://www.facebook.com/thebulldidntwin/

First printing: Date July 2021
ISBN-13: 978-1-951451-05-9 (paper)
ISBN-13: 978-1-951451-06-6 (eBook)
ISBN-13: 978-1-951451-04-2 (hardback)
ISBN-13: 978-1-951451-07-3 (audio)

Printed in the United States of America

Disclaimer: The contents of this book, such as text, graphics, images, and other material is for entertainment purposes only.

Dedication

This book is dedicated to all who prayed for Jacob and helped our family. A special thanks to Dr. Drew Davis, Skibo Holman, Marianne McCray, Beth Randall, Dr. Kelvie Culpepper, Dr. Peter Keen, Sean Hiller, Payton McBryde, Ali Hathcock, Dana Edins, teachers, and all of the staff at Children's Hospital of Birmingham.

Table of Contents

"God's going to take you so many places in your life,
so never take your eyes off of Him."

—Susan Browder

"Whatever your bull is in life, don't let it win."

—Jacob Browder

"When you put your hope and trust in something bigger than
you, be prepared to be blown away."

—Susan Browder

About The Authors

My name is Jacob Browder. I am a love-every-moment-of-your-life kind of man. I live life to its fullest and I have mastered the skill of perseverance AND the phrase "put one foot in front of the other." I have a never give up attitude, which has pushed me to reach my goals. I do not take "no's" very often, which has unquestionably been in my favor. I have a degree in Machine Tool Technology, which I am not currently using. I own my own landscaping business Browder Lawncare. I am in the process of buying cattle. I am twenty-two years old. I took taxidermy courses where I learned how to mount deer. I go to a physical therapy rehab facility to continue to build strength, coordination, and reach numerous goals. I plan on writing another book.

My name is Susan Browder. I am a public-school teacher and have just started my twenty-fifth year. I love my job and passing on my knowledge in a passionate manner. I get paid to spend my time with children, and I am honored to do it. I teach an adult Bible studies class to seasoned adults. My mom instilled in me at a very early age to love with my whole heart and to protect the ones you love. My most honored job is being a mom and grandmother. There is nothing more rewarding, and it absolutely fills my heart up. I have a husband, Nicky, who raises catfish. I have another son, Nick, who is married to Mallory. I have a granddaughter, Nixon Lyn, and a grandson, Baker Gray. I love spending time on the river with my family.

Chapter One

Getting Started

When I first started rodeoing, a verse from Deuteronomy spoke to me. Deuteronomy 31:6 says, "Be strong and courageous. Do not fear or be in dread of them, for it is the LORD your God who goes with you. He will not leave you nor forsake you." (ESV) Little did I know where this verse would take me, what it would mean to my family and me, and the hope it would give us. [1]

As a little kid from Alabama who would catch snakes and do anything dangerous that anyone said I wouldn't do, I had always wanted to be a bull rider. From riding on the arm of the couch pretending it was a bull, to being on the back of an untamed wild animal, I was determined to make that happen. I was an adrenaline junkie, and I would ride the mechanical bull at rodeos when I was little. I used to picture myself being in a rodeo.

The rules in bull riding require a rope be tightened just behind the front shoulders of the bull; someone pulls the rope tight until your hand is tied to the bull's back, while the other arm is free.

---

[1] King James Bible (Deuteronomy, 31;6) Biblehub. https://biblehub.com/deuteronomy /31-6.htm

You use your free arm to balance yourself on the back of the bull, and you're not allowed to touch the bull with your free arm.

There is another rope tied on the bull's flank, called a flank strap. This rope makes him buck and try to kick the strap off. I also had a pair of spurs on each boot. I used the spurs to get a hold with my feet and legs too. You also could spur the bull for extra points. My favorite movie growing up was and still is, *8 Seconds*. I have seen this movie at least a thousand times. If you haven't seen it, it is a must.

When I was four years old, I was the mutton bustin champion at a rodeo in my hometown. This is where all the kids at the rodeo get to enter to see who gets the most points on the fastest sheep that runs out of the chute. I won this contest, and I was on cloud nine with my medal and first-place trophy.

When I turned 14, I figured I was big enough to start getting on some bulls. I got in touch with one of my old hometown friends that I knew rode bulls a little. He invited me to a rodeo arena in Selma, Alabama, where a few people went to practice. My mother drove me, and we met him and followed him to the arena. When we got there, I stepped out of the car and got this nervous feeling down in me that I have rarely felt. This was an experience I had never had before. It was almost hard to breathe, and I started sweating, but moments later, excitement kicked in.

We walked over to this lady who was making everyone sign a waiver that said if you get crushed, stomped, or "kilt," they were not to be sued. I kind of knew it was a joke, but my mom's eyes lit up like "are you kidding me?" I watched a few guys ride, and it pumped me up. It was finally my turn. I was so nervous crawling down in the bucking chute for the first time, and to be honest, I was a little scared too. If a bull rider has ever told you, "I'm never scared," he's telling you a bald face lie.

I slid my hand in my rope; one of the bull riders pulled it tight. I squeezed the bull tight with my legs and nodded as if I was ready. The young bull came bucking out of the chute and bucked halfway across the arena. I stayed on the bull for at least eight seconds. I made my dismount, and I went over to all the cowboys behind the bucking chutes. I high fived them and celebrated, and then we headed home. My mom and dad thought it was just a one-time thing, but that wasn't the case. I was ready to get on another bull the next day.

I spent a whole week talking with my mom about bull riding while she was cooking each night in the kitchen. All I got from my mom was, "You are not riding another bull, Jacob Browder." So I realized I was going to have to work on my dad with the whole situation. I thought maybe I could get him to sway my mom a little. Well, let's just say it took plenty of convincing and I got a lot of mad mama looks, but she finally gave in. I wanted to do it again and we agreed that if I was going to do it, I was going to be all in or all out.

One day, I remember I got on my horse pretending he was a bull, putting all my weight on my legs with my free arm up and my other hand holding on. Bowing my chest out and keeping my head down, I would just get the horse to lope in circles. This was a good training method some people who ride bulls use. I couldn't just get on bulls whenever I wanted to, so my dad and I also built a bucking barrel in the backyard. It was a blue fifty-five gallon drum with ropes attached to each end and springs to buck like a bull would. I would get on the bucking barrel to practice because it was the closest thing to an actual bull.

Chapter Two

Where He Has Taken Me

I have been taken so many places in my life where I have felt tremendous heartbreak. I lost my mom when I was twenty-three years old. She was only forty-eight. My mom was always there for it all. She was my biggest cheerleader, favorite person of my friends and all who met her, my bully fighter, my son's biggest fan, and the list could go on. The pain and loss I felt the day she died has never stopped.

You see, you never really think about how much you will always need your mom, especially when you are young and dumb and take her for granted. September 6, 2014 was the day I needed my mom most. It was a day that changed our lives forever. It was a day the pain I described doubled because I didn't have my mom to grab me and comfort me.

I got married young and had a son, Nick. Nick was an easy child to raise. My husband, Nicky, and I always looked at each other when other parents were complaining about their children and how difficult and chaotic it was raising them. We couldn't relate. Nick was a super easy laidback child, and for the most part, never had to learn things the hard way. He usually took our word when we told him not to do something or gave him advice. Six years later, I had my son, Jacob. He was the exact opposite. He had to learn almost everything the hard way, he had to cross nearly every line, and he had to do it his way.

I will never forget his first rodeo. He was one. He was dressed in his wranglers and his brother's handed down red boots. He was the cutest cowboy, and he was so still in the stands, taking in all that was around him. He didn't have to be at a rodeo to wear his red boots. He wore them with everything.

As Jacob grew up, my days were filled with finding him, running from him chasing me with real live snakes, going as fast as he could in anything that could move, and his love for the outdoors. While most kids were watching cartoons or movies, Jacob was watching the outdoor channel and rodeo.

I always knew I was in trouble when he had another one of his ideas just by the way he said, "Mama." There was always a different and serious tone when he said my name, and he had something to let me in on that he knew I was not going to be thrilled about. I will never forget the day he ran upstairs to find me and tell me he wanted to go to a practice pen and ride a bull. Jacob is always pulling my leg, so this I really thought was a joke.

After a few minutes of realizing he was serious, I gave him my answer in an all caps voice, "ABSOLUTELY NOT." I could feel my blood rushing, my face turning red, and my voice was going too fast to keep up with my thoughts. At this moment, I was thinking to myself, *Lord, we really don't want to go down this road, do we?* I've seen all the rodeo movies, watched countless rodeo wrecks, and seen some heartbreaking moments. Bull riding is an unpredictable sport, and you are pretty much guaranteed to get hurt at some point. A bull is a massive animal, and outweighs a person tremendously. I just didn't want my son to be put in a situation where he could lose his life or get severely injured. I didn't want to be that parent who lost their child or whose child experienced a change in their life due to this sport. Why couldn't we just continue to play football, baseball, basketball, go hunting and fishing? But anything my sons have wanted to do in life, I have always tried to make happen.

Well three weeks later, we ended up in the bullpen. We walked up into an arena full of people who I didn't know, and I was about to trust them with my son. I saw a man drinking a shot of whiskey. I don't drink whiskey, but I sure could have used a sip at this time. A very country lady approached me and explained to me she didn't have a waiver on her, but we could do a "verbal" one. She said, "Ma'am, do you understand that your son can get stomped on, bucked off, rolled on, or even kilt?"

As it became Jacob's turn to ride, my eyes widened as Jimmy, the bull riding coach, yelled out my son's name. When I got to him, I tried to reason with him and change his mind. As he zipped up another rider's chest protector and slid on her helmet, I prayed for Jacob to chicken out, but that did not happen. Jacob rode the bull, and I witnessed a look in his eye that I had never seen. He rode another bull and the look was still there. As he walked over to me, I heard that different tone in his voice when he said my name. "Mama," he said. "Mama, I love it." But he didn't have to tell me. It was written all over his face.

As we rode home and talked, I said, "Jacob, why in the world would you want to ride a bull?" As Jacob began to give me his reasons and listed them, he tugged at my heartstrings. Jacob said, "Mom, I have always felt like I have been in my brother's shadow, and I feel like rodeo is a way to break away from that and make my own path. You know the look Nick gets in his eyes when he plays football? I think that is how I feel about rodeo. I think I love it."

Chapter Three

My First Event

After I started riding, a few weeks went by and I heard about the Alabama high school rodeo association, the AHSRA, and I wanted to join. The first rodeo of the year was in Andalusia, Alabama. It was about a three-hour drive to Andalusia from where we lived. The rodeo was at 7 p.m. and it was indoors at Garrett Coliseum. I had to pick my contestant number up at the front desk. I remember the lady asking for my name and I said, "Jacob Browder." She handed me my number and it read twenty-one in big bold numbers. This was my number for the rest of the year, at every rodeo. She also handed me a piece of paper with the number of the tag that was in the bull's ear. I went looking for the tag that said number sixty-four. After looking at a few bulls, I finally found the right one and my eyes got wide. I hated to imagine my mom's reaction when she saw the bull I drew. He was the biggest bull in the pen. He was strong, and white with black spots. One ugly word in particular came to my mind, and it rhymes with "it." I froze and was very unsure because he was much more than I thought or wanted him to be.

It felt like forever sitting through all of the team roping and barrel racing. The nervousness built up, but I was ready. As I was down behind the bucking chutes putting rosin on my rope, getting it hot and sticky so that my hand didn't come out, I heard, "Load 'em up!" One bull ran into the first chute, then another one ran into the second chute; that was my bull. I went over to him and hooked my bull rope around him as I watched the first rider get out. He bucked off pretty quick and the bull stepped on him numerous times. He was taken by ambulance because it was pretty clear he had some broken bones. Knowing I was the next rider out stirred my nerves up. As I slid down on my bull, I had a guy talking in my ear to pump me up, but I wasn't even listening. I was so focused. All I could think was, *this is my first real bull riding event.*

I put my hand in my bull rope, and some guy pulled my rope tight. I got up on my rope and nodded my head saying, "Let's go, boys!" The bull came out bucking and turned into a spin. I stayed with him a few bucks and spins, but he was so powerful. He was a little too much for me. What happened next was not at all what I was hoping for. The bull bucked me off and I found myself underneath him. As his powerful back legs thrust into my rib cage and back, I felt an extreme pain in my ribs that I had never felt before. It felt like a mac truck rammed into me. For the first time in my life, I felt like I couldn't breathe. I honestly felt like I was going to collapse and hit the ground from the piercing pain. I was doing all that I could to stand on my feet. I kept putting my hands over my head, gasping for air. The cowboys behind the chutes waved for the ambulance to come into the arena. I finally caught my breath as they loaded me onto a stretcher and up into the ambulance. I knew that something was broken in that instant.

The ambulance took me to the hospital in Andalusia, and when we arrived, we learned that I had broken six ribs and I had fractured my transverse vertebras. They kept me in the hospital for a few nights before I went home to heal up. A few weeks went by and I wanted to pick up a new sport since I had to give bull riding a rest for a bit. Coach Massey approached me about playing high school tennis, and I liked the idea of doing something new. I remember the conversation with my mom like it was yesterday. She came in from teaching school and I said, "Hey, Mom, is tennis a safe enough sport for you?" That question didn't get an ugly or a crazy look! It got the most surprised and relieved expression from my mom. She said, "I can handle that one, son." So instead of sitting on the edge of her seat at a rodeo, she got to sit in her lawn chair and chill while watching me play tennis.

At the end of the season, my tennis team had a banquet, and my coach was recognizing players. When he got to me, he said, "This guy just might be the only person in the state of Alabama that plays football, tennis, and rides bulls." The crowd in the room busted out laughing. At that moment, I felt like a proud, all-around athlete. I knew that I couldn't give the sport of bull riding up that easy. Now that tennis season had ended, spring rolled around, and I talked with my parents about letting me ride bulls again.

"Hey, Mom, let's get back to bull riding again." Of course, she didn't like that thought. "Hey, Dad, what do you think? Is it time to start training again?" Dad started looking at bull riding schools and trying to find a good one near our town. After a lot of thought and discussion, my mom said, "Being the daredevil that you are, I know you are going to ride bulls anyway when you get older, so start making plans to ride again." My parents decided to support me instead of taking it away from me. My dad said, "You will have to go to rodeo schools to learn more about being the bull rider that you want to be and to learn the right techniques to keep you as safe as possible." I was willing to do whatever it took.

Chapter Four

Where He has Taken Me

The next few years were filled with the Browders packing up the Jeep with rodeo equipment almost every weekend. In his first high school event, right off the bat, he was thrown under the bull and flown to Children's Hospital of Alabama. He had broken ribs, a bruised kidney, and his transverse vertebras were broken. We spent three days at the hospital, and his brother, Nick, was by his side the entire time. Nick listened to the physical therapist and doctors and made Jacob do what he needed to do in order to recover. My heart was full to see how concerned Nick was for his little brother and how he walked him up and down the hall. At this time, Nick was in college and taking classes to be in the education field like me. I noticed as he was helping Jacob throughout the day, he was enjoying it and really getting into it. Nick sat down and was very quiet. Moments later he said, "Mom, I need to talk to you." This is usually a sit-down moment because he doesn't say this often. He said, "I have a burning in my chest." I was like, oh my goodness, do you need a Pepcid? He looked at me and shook his head, and said, "Mom, I do not mean heartburn… I mean, I think I know what I want to do with my life. I think I want to be a physical therapist." Helping Jacob nudged him towards a different field of study. As I wrapped my brain around this one, we began to wrap up our time there and head home to help Jacob recover for a few weeks. I thought we were probably done with rodeoing, but I was so wrong.

We traveled all over Alabama, to Florida, Georgia, and to Texas. One of my favorite memories of Jacob riding was a hot day in July. He was in Tuscaloosa, Alabama, and placed second; later the same day, we drove a couple of hours to Weptumka, Alabama, where he rode and got a first-place win! The look on his face after these two wins on the same day was a moment that cannot be put into

words. The best way I know to describe it was he was entirely too much to handle. He ripped off his wrangle button shirt and was exceptionally proud. Today, people would describe this as being "extra." He was absolutely extra on this day.

Chapter Five

Best Of Times To My Worst Nightmare

My dad and I found out about a rodeo school happening in Georgia that weekend. We made the five-hour drive, and it had been a few months since I had been on my last bull. I was really itching to get back on. The first bull I was getting on at "Sankey Rodeo School" was white with brown spots. As I lowered myself down into the chute, my dad pulled my rope tight. As I scooted myself up on my rope, a rush of thoughts flooded through my head about my last bull wreck. As I nodded, the gate opened, and I was so nervous I wasn't thinking. I didn't have a hold with my legs! After a few big jumps, the bull bucked me off, but my hand hung up in the rope. He carried me halfway across the arena, bucking and spinning. The bullfighters got my hand out, but not until after they took some shots from the bull. I got on some more bulls that weekend and met some really good people, even a lifelong best friend. I learned a lot at the school and was ready to enter some more rodeos and put my hard work and techniques to use. I took a break from high school rodeos and started entering some hometown rodeos with some buddies.

One of my best memories in my bull riding career was when I won second one afternoon at a rodeo in Tuscaloosa, Alabama. Afterwards, my traveling partners and I jumped in the truck and hightailed it to Wetumpka, Alabama, which was a little over two hours, and I was blessed enough to win first that night. I had no idea how good I had it when all I had to do was wake up and wonder when the next rodeo was. I didn't know just how short my bull riding career would be.

There were rodeos in other states that my traveling partners and I went to. In some, I placed, and in others, they did. We were invited to the world finals in Abilene, Texas in July of 2014. The bulls at the world finals were no joke. I had never seen anything like them. I can remember climbing down into the chutes, just sitting there watching, taking it all in, realizing where I was. I was so proud of myself. It was a great experience, and a good time was had by all. I had the opportunity to ride four bulls, but came up short. I was excited and blessed that I got to ride with the best cowboys around. Little did I know, this would be the last rodeo.

Texas was fun and a good experience for the Bama boys: KJ, Ethan, Nace, and Robert. I called us the Bama boys since we were all from Alabama. I met these boys in Selma, Alabama, and we had been riding together for a few years. We all went to the World Finals in Abilene, Texas together, and I got a buckle for qualifying. I had a little work to do to get better, though. I went back home and went straight to the practice pen. I rode a few good bulls and then started football.

Chapter Six

Where He Has Taken Me

School started back up and Jacob started playing football while he still practiced and went to rodeo schools. On September 5, 2014, around 3:00 p.m., Jacob was on the bus with the football team headed to Calera, Alabama. I was doing what a teacher always does on a Friday afternoon. I was straightening up my classroom and getting things ready for the next week. Normally, my co-teacher and I would plan on a weekly basis for our math classes, but lately, we had decided to plan two weeks ahead of time. Even after doing this extra, I felt the need to get more plans together for more than this time frame. For some reason, this day seemed in slow motion to me. I remember how I was a little late changing my calendar on my bulletin board, so I quickly placed September on the board and rearranged the dates to get my calendar up to date. As I turned off the lights to my classroom and glanced around at how in order everything was, I had a feeling of peace at leaving, knowing all was ready for the week. Little did I know how out of order and not peaceful my life was about to become.

Chapter Seven

One More Bull

My football team had an away game on September 5, 2014 in Calera, Alabama. When the game was over, I went into the locker room to change. As I slipped my jeans on, they felt a little lighter than before the game. Moments later, I realized my wallet was no longer in my pocket. I looked around for it, and out of the corner of my eye, I saw it on the floor. It was empty. All of my money from placing in rodeos had vanished. I was so angry. Of course, when the coach looked into it and asked, no one raised their hand or came forward to admit they took it.

My mom and I left the game, and we were off to another rodeo school to get better. We arrived in Montgomery, where the rodeo school was, and my dad showed up to watch me. There were a lot of drills that we did before we got to put our new style of riding together. I rode the hair off of the first bull and my mom thought that I was done for the night.

She was packing the car up, and I went over to her and my dad and asked them if I could get on one more bull. She gave me the "are you kidding me?" look, the one that I have seen a lot in my lifetime. The bull loaded in the bucking chute was named E.W. Everyone knew that this bull was really bad at getting riders on the end of their riding arm and jerking them down over his head on his first couple of jumps out of the chute. I lowered myself down into the chute and eased my way down on the back of E.W. I took my wrap, slid up, and nodded. What happened next, my mom will have to tell you because I have no memory of it.

Chapter Eight

Where He Has Taken Me

All of the parents were invited to watch the end of the rodeo school where we could see the bull riders show off all of their hard work. Jacob rode his bull, and I packed up the Jeep. We were all ready to go when Jacob walked, bowlegged, over to me with that look in his eye. The one that means he's about to talk me into something. And that smile that leads with his sweet voice, "Mama." He wanted to get on another bull, and he pointed at it. It was massive, and other riders were talking about this bull E.W., and how he was known for kicking high. In a nutshell, he was bad.

I felt like Jacob was looking to me to really say no. He looked a little unsure, and I had not seen that look much when it came to doing dangerous things. I told him absolutely not. A few minutes later, Jacob was on E.W.

E.W. came out of the chute like a mad man. I remember it like it happened moments ago. Jacob stayed with him on the first buck. The second buck was a little different. The bull got Jacob stretched out on the end of his arm and jerked him down; they collided heads. His hand was still in the rope and he was still sitting up. He bucked again; the bull's head was going up as he was coming down. They head-butted again and he was knocked out cold.

I remember how high he kicked his back legs and how he was almost standing straight up on his front legs. I am not sure if you can grasp what it is like for a mom to watch her son do something like ride bulls. In all of my videos, I am saying the same thing. When Jacob gets bucked off and falls down, you can hear me shouting, "Get up." On this video, you can't hear me shout those words. The biggest storm of my life was blowing through.

As we all ran into the arena, the other riders kept assuring me they had seen this before and it was not unheard of. They kept saying, "He'll come to." My husband, Nicky, took off his cracked helmet and he was bleeding. There was an eerie and unusual feeling surrounding us. It reminded me of the scene in, *The Passion of the Christ* where Jesus is being beaten and Satan is lurking in the crowd.

I felt evil prowling inside the arena. It was the most terrible atmosphere to be surrounded by. Jacob's belly did a strange rolling motion, and he did not wake up. I begged every cowboy and parent to start praying, and a young man started a prayer out loud. I did not have cell service and asked the lady who was hosting the riding school to call nine-one-one. She hesitated and said to give him a few more minutes. Nicky doesn't usually panic or shed tears, but at this moment of helplessness, he did. Nicky yelled, "Somebody who has service, call right now."

It was so difficult to look at my full-of-life son now completely unconscious. The ambulance arrived, and as the paramedics assessed him, we heard the words, "He has a severe brain injury, and we need to call for life flight." Nicky and I were put in the back of a police car that followed the ambulance and took Jacob to a nearby clearing where the helicopter landed. Nicky got out of the police car. I froze. I sat there peering out of the car with my eyes on my son as he was being intubated. I could not move. It didn't feel real. Then I felt a need to be right beside my son, holding his hand, and I went to open the back door of the police car, but it was locked. I banged, screamed, and called out to unlock the door, but no one heard me.

He was flown to the local Montgomery hospital, where we got to see him. Nicky, the group of people at the rodeo school, and I waited in the waiting room for someone to come in and speak with us. I remember how angry I was at my husband at this time. He tried to hug and comfort me and I pushed him away. I blamed him for the accident. He made all of the rodeo stuff possible for Jacob. He got all of the equipment, training, and scheduled the rodeos and schools. I was so upset with him, but all he was doing was believing in Jacob and making Jacob's dream of rodeo come true. He wanted Jacob to pursue rodeo because he saw how happy it made him. That is all a father wants for his son, to live a life pursuing his dreams.

The next moment, I did something I had never done before. I kneeled and put my face to the floor to pray. I went to the feet of Jesus. I wanted God to know I believed He is above all things and He can do anything. I found myself in a place I had never been. I felt so broken and weighed down with guilt for not protecting my child. It was a heavy sense of responsibility. I have experienced heartbreak before, but this kind was very different. My reaction was not to scream or cry. I couldn't control the situation we were all in. I continued to talk to God over and over again, not caring who heard me or what they thought.

As the doctors came in, we were quickly told he would be flown to Children's Hospital of Birmingham. I called my sisters, dad, and aunt. Then I called my friend, Trish, who before I knew it, was there with her family. We left to go to Birmingham by car, and Trish and her family stayed with Jacob while the staff got him ready to be transported.

Nicky put the hazard lights on, and we flew to Birmingham until we were pulled over by two policemen. They did not at all care to hear about why we were going so fast or that we were told to put our hazard lights on by the people transporting Jacob. They kept us several minutes and finally let us go on our way.

As we were driving, the song, "I'm Already There," by Lonestar came on. I could barely hold myself together. Anytime my boys call me needing me to be there for them or needing my help, it's an immediate drop everything feeling. I want them to feel as if I'm already there. *Mama's on the way, but she's already there in spirit praying over you and asking the Lord to intervene.* I was praying Jacob felt this from me in these moments. I wanted my son to feel as though I was sitting right beside him.

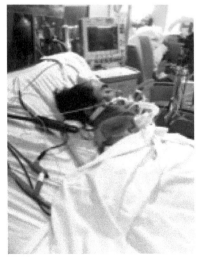

We arrived at the hospital and were instantly taken to be with Jacob. When we got to him, he was completely covered in tubes. A few hours later, we received the news no parents want to hear. We were told he had five bleeds in his brain, he was in a coma, and had a Diffuse Axonal Injury, a DAI. A DAI is a form of traumatic brain injury with widespread trauma and damage involving shearing and tearing of the axons of the brain. It happens when the brain rapidly shifts and moves inside the skull during an accident. We were told the next thirty-six hours were critical, and that if he didn't wake up by the thirty-six-hour timeline, he probably wouldn't wake up. If he did, the prognosis was not good.

Chapter Nine

Where He Has Taken Me

I don't know if you have ever sat right beside an unconscious loved one, holding their hand. If not, I hope you never have to, especially your child. Not knowing if they will wake up, or what happens next is a very scary, helpless feeling. As we waited by Jacob's bedside, we talked to him, prayed over him, and cried. The next day came quickly, and as the sun went down and darkness came, the twenty-four-hour period had passed. I was spiraling because my son had not shown any sign of waking up. I am very literal and watched the clock. I knew by the thirty-sixth hour Jacob would come back to us. As a mom, you can't see it any other way. I was one hundred percent incorrect. As the clock was a few minutes shy of the time we were told he should wake up, I started yelling at Jacob. In my mind, if I yelled, he would hear me and come out of this. I am his mom, so surely; he would hear me.

Nicky came over to where I was and touched my arm, telling me to stop. I was so mad at myself for allowing this to happen to Jacob. The whys started flooding in, and then blame set in. Why did I allow him to do rodeo? Why didn't I just say no? Why did I sign a waiver? Shouldn't signing a waiver be a flag to any parent? This was all my fault, so I was not going to stop praying and making everyone do what they were supposed to do until Jacob was Jacob again.

Children's Hospital became our home. Nicky slept on the built-in hospital couch; I slept on an air mattress. My son, Nick, and his girlfriend at the time but now his wife Mallory, came every day they could. They were both in college. My cousin Nikki and cousin's wife, Justin, as well as my aunt, were there early almost every morning to be present when the doctors made their rounds. Nikki and Justin were both nurses, so they knew better questions to ask. We had many friends there daily, like Lisa. She covered us with food and her time.

The first few days were really tough just waiting. Doctors would come in and grab Jacob's chest. They would twist his skin in hopes of getting what they call, "purposeful movement." Nothing happened. I remember how loudly they called his name, seeing if there was any reaction. This was the daily routine each morning. After a week, the doctors came in to do this another time. This time, I saw movement and started crying and jumping. Jacob drew his hands in, turning them and pulling them up towards his chest. Filled with happiness, joy, and relief, Nicky and I looked around at the doctors and noticed they weren't as excited. I asked them, "Did you see that?" The doctors then explained to us what those types of movements were. They called it posturing, and explained that it wasn't a purposeful movement but indicated severe damage to the brain. There was so much being said by doctors at this time, and most of the information I had no idea what they were talking about or what it all meant. I was waiting for the good and positive information because that was something I desperately needed to hear.

After this moment, I began to like some doctors, but not care for others. I am a question asker, so at this time, I was firing anything at them. I remember one doctor coming in while my sister, Rhonda, was visiting, and my cousin Nikki was there with us. I looked at Jacob and asked the doctor what he thought was going to happen.

As the doctor pointed towards Jacob, he said something I did not accept. He said Jacob could be just as he was in this moment for the rest of his life. My response to him was that if he wasn't going to be positive, he could leave. My cousin Nikki followed him out the door. Being a nurse, she knew doctors usually told the worst-case scenario. She explained to the doctor that we needed to be positive and to hear another option. The doctor came back in and apologized then told me, "We just don't know; traumatic brain injuries are different for everyone."

A few days passed, and Jacob needed a needle placed in his head to relieve the pressure inside. A nurse came in to shave the spot where it would be placed. We waited outside as the procedure was done. The procedure was lightning fast, and we were back with Jacob within minutes. It was another tube going into my son to add with all the others, but this one was a little scarier to me.

It was difficult to hear the same morning script read aloud by the resident doctor as the doctors made their rounds. It started off as, "This is Jacob Browder. He was injured in a bull riding accident. He has Diffuse Axonal Injury. His numbers are not what we want." Day to day, other things were added. I got really tired of hearing the reason we were here with not many positive comments. I just wanted to hear something different. So, I covered Jacob's hospital door in photos. I wanted every medical person who entered Jacob's room

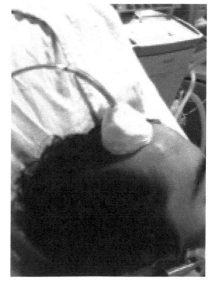

to see who he was. I didn't want them only to look at him as an unconscious person who might or might not wake up. I wanted them to see a full-of-life young man who had his whole life in front of him. I wanted them to see that he did so many things like played football, loved to fish, hunt, spend time on the river and with his family.

Every day, I got up and kept a positive mindset. Jacob's friends, family, coaches, teachers, football team, and other bull riders continued to visit. They all arrived with hugs and sad looks in their eyes, and most of them were in tears as they left Jacob's room. As we prepared for the rest of the week, we were told Jacob would be taken into surgery to have screws placed in where his mandible was broken. This was something I had forgotten about because it had taken a backseat to all of his other injuries. I can't begin to fully describe what it is like to turn your unconscious son over to be operated on when he has so many things going on in his body. I was a wreck,

and finally had to be told it was time to take him. The hospital staff was so kind and let us back to wait with Jacob. Everyone was in the room preparing when soon the staff started staring at Nicky and I with the look of when are they leaving? As I sat down and waited, I read Philippians 4:6-7, "Don't worry about anything; instead, pray about everything. Tell God what you need and thank him for all he has done.

Then you will experience God's peace, which exceeds anything we can understand. His peace will guard your hearts and minds as you live in Christ Jesus." (NLT) This has always been my favorite verse, but little did I know how much I would need these words. In this moment, this verse meant for me to tell God EVERYTHING I needed, give it to him, and all I had to do was to keep on having faith, trust Him, and not worry about the outcome because God's got this! I had never fully comprehended what it meant to tell God all that I needed. It was a tall order that I asked of God and the peace that I experienced in return was its reflection. [23]

This is the same day a friend brought me a journal. We were part of a small town and connected through our love for the Lord. We were not close friends, but she reached out to me one night knowing that I needed something that I didn't even know I needed at the time. I needed an outlet and a way to get my thoughts down, write about what I was grateful for, progress that was made, and frustrations I felt. This journal gave me the opportunity to express my prayers, hopes, and scariest moments on paper. Later, I was able to look back at something so powerful. That's the great thing about my journal. It reminded me of all that I went through, how I was feeling in that moment, and it shows the power of healing and God taking care of us all.

As I sat beside Jacob, praying for him to wake up from his coma, I slid my hand across this light blue journal and found myself quickly opening it to write down all I was experiencing. Writing helped me get all I was feeling out on this blue lined paper and brought me to the place I desperately needed to be. What I didn't know at the time was what this journal would mean to me much later.

---

[2] King James Bible (Philippians, 4:6) Biblehub. https://biblehub.com/philippians/4-6.htm
[3] King James Bible (Philippians, 4:7) Biblehub.https://biblehub.com/philippians/4-7.htm

Over the next few weeks, I heard stories of people doing some amazing things for us. We are part of two different communities. We raised our boys in Moundville, Alabama, but we moved to Demopolis, Alabama in 2012. These two communities started two different t-shirt orders to raise money for my family. On one shirt, people had their choice of pink or grey, and it said, "Praying for Jacob" with a picture of a bull rider. The second shirt was blue because blue was Jacob's favorite color. This shirt said, "In Jesus Name We Ride," like the bracelet Jacob always wore on his wrist.

I began to get so many texts, calls, and Facebook messages. Students were writing papers on Jacob. Students were doing projects on him. Jacob's friend, Justin, had "Ride Like JB Would" stitched on his sleeve. Students setting up lemonade stands. Communities doing trail rides. People were sending me messages of funny stories of Jacob. Some stories he was lucky he was in a coma for because

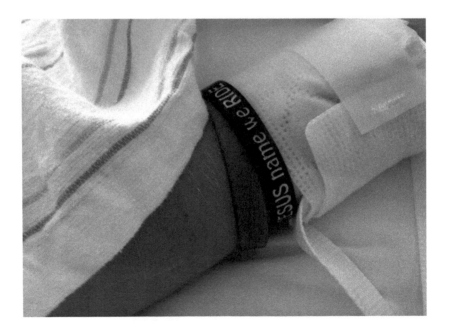

they involved things we didn't know about but can laugh about now. This was very helpful to me as a mom, to know others cared enough about him to do this.

As we were in the hospital, life was going on in the world we used to live in. I got texts and calls every morning, and I always got my regular texts and calls from my friends Trish, Jennifer, and Johna. Trish was holding down the fort at school and running my classroom and hers. Jennifer continued to go on our 5:00 a.m. walks, and she texted me saying the dogs were looking for me. Her dogs Chaco and Maya always met me in the same place at the top of her road, waiting on me to greet them and go with us. Johna wasn't her normal bubbly self that kept us all in stitches. All of these ladies' hearts were right there with me. And I knew they hurt for me.

Day after day, we continued to pray. Another cousin, Craig, visited us several times. Craig knows the Bible like the back of his hand. Craig asked permission to Read James 5 in the room with Jacob and us. There were about five of us in the room. I had never seen Craig so serious.

Before Craig read James 5, he said, "It is important to confess our sins when praying James 5." So Craig gave us all a moment to pray and ask for forgiveness. We all formed a circle and prayed. I can remember thinking of every sin I had ever committed down to the Tootsie Roll I stole as a child. I prayed for God to forgive me for all of them, and even the ones I could not think of. I remember in the middle of James 5, a nurse entered the room. Craig stopped in his tracks and paused from reading. He said, "Everybody wait." After the nurse left, Craig continued reading word for word from James 5. This was my first "Holy Spirit" experience. He was in the room with us. I absolutely know this because it was the most powerful moment I have ever felt in my life. It was a moment that really can't be described to its fullest. It was powerful and the most perfect communication. It was a feeling of peace and that someone else was now in control. It was so important during our time to only have people in the room who had repented and who believed what James 5 says.

Two days later, we woke up to what looked like Jacob peeking through his eyelids. It was a very tiny peek, but it was a peek. I ran and got everyone. Each day that passed, Jacob's eyes opened a little more. This was the smallest thing to most, but it was the biggest thing to me. I could see his eyes, and that is all it took. Then I looked down at the bracelet on Jacob's wrist. It was white with black writing and it read, "In Jesus Name We Ride." This changed my mind set.

That night, I listened to some music, and the song "Live Like You Were Dying" by Tim McGraw came on. As I listened, I related in so many ways to the words because this is how Jacob lived every day. He lived and got everything out of every day and didn't fear anything. I reflected on the moment that stopped him on a dime. So, I thought then and there how much life he had in front of him and I prayed for him to have the opportunity to continue to grow up and experience all he wanted to.

When you are in a hospital for an extended period of time, you start to feel the walls close in. I would constantly watch all the numbers on the monitors and look for the heart rate, oxygen levels, and other numbers. So, I tried to quiet all of the beeping, doors opening and closing, voices, and other noises around me. I started to think about how overwhelming this process has been, but also how close I had felt to the Lord. I also thought about all the times I turned away from God when I faced adversity. Each time I turned away from Him, everything crumbled. So, I knew now, that was the last thing I needed. I felt a pull towards God that gave me trust and faith that was much bigger than I have ever known. He helped me face Jacob's daily hurdles that seemed as if they would never end.

The next day, Jacob started following commands. This was huge! It meant he understood what we were asking him! Now we were able to communicate! The nurse asked Jacob if he could hear her and we got our first thumbs up! I am a person who is a huge fan of the thumbs up, and I probably do it twenty times a day. But this thumbs up meant so much! It meant Jacob could comprehend and understand what was being said and answer the questions. This brought so much hope to us all.

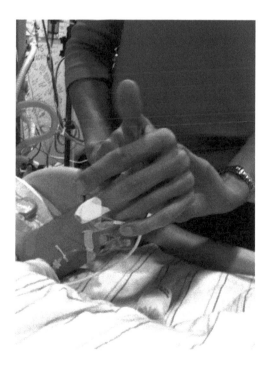

Chapter Ten

Waking Up

A Facebook page was created, and it was called "Praying for Jacob." That's where updates were posted so people could know what was going on. Doctors figured out that since I hit the left side of my head, the right side of my body was damaged. This meant that my right side would be weaker than my left side. I do not remember being in a coma and just lying there, but I do remember not being able to move or even open my eyes at some point. I remember hearing my parents and the nurses coming to check on me in the middle of the night, but I felt like it was all a bad dream. The bad dream continued, and I didn't know what was going on because I didn't remember anything that put me in the hospital. At this time, I was super confused as to what was going on. I could follow directions when told to do something, but my eyes were still closed.

At the start of the third week of being in a coma, I had a little peek in my eyes like I was trying to wake up. That peek got wider and wider each day, and after a few times of my mom saying, "Open those big blue eyes," I finally did it! I opened my eyes, but I still couldn't talk.

Chapter Eleven

Where He Has Taken Me

When I was a little girl, each year in early December, my Aunt Tricia would schedule it with my mom for my sisters and me to come over and make Christmas Cookies. My aunt's recipe for these sugar cookies was a "from scratch" recipe. It was very detailed, lots of fun, and a lengthy process. It was the best of times! These cookies were the best cookies I had ever eaten. They still are to this day. I think the reason was because of how much harder they were to make than regular box or premade dough cookies. There was a great deal of time involved in making them, so we anticipated them and worked them up in our heads all day. Then we got to decorate them!

I have done so many things in my life "from scratch." Things that were certainly not easy and took way more time than I hoped they would. Doing life's "from scratch" version isn't as much fun, and it doesn't taste as sweet in the middle. So, doing cookies from scratch didn't prepare me for starting Jacob's fifteen-year-old life from scratch.

I remember looking at Jacob when he woke up from his coma. He couldn't talk, walk, eat, drink, or anything else. He just laid there on a ventilator with his eyes peeking through the slenderest peep hole. Each day the doctors came in, I was hoping this was the day he was strong enough to get the ventilator removed. These days just kept going by, and the one positive doctor we had used words I will never forget. She said, "I want to give Jacob a chance. One more day and I think he has a chance to survive. He isn't strong enough today."

So, the next day, this doctor came in and she told us it was today! As she took Jacob off the ventilator, I buried my head into Nicky's chest. Moments later, Nicky patted me, and I heard a very quiet, "He's breathing." The next words are the words that really stuck with me and drove me daily. The doctor went on to tell us that all traumatic brain injuries are different; she was hopeful, but stressed the words "relearn" and "from scratch" to us. She basically told us Jacob would have to learn everything all over again and start from scratch just like when he was a baby.

I knew this "from scratch" was going to be the most difficult recipe I have ever whipped up. So, every day, I woke up with a "this is what we are going to do today" attitude. No matter how small, I made a huge deal out of everything that happened. If it wasn't a positive, I turned it into one. Remember, I am a teacher, and you know teachers love a chart. I grabbed some markers and asked a nurse for some chart paper. I wrote down everything that Jacob had done. I wrote down any kind of movements, such as eyes moved, eyes twitched, eyes followed, leg flopped off of the bed, and even a bowel movement. No matter what it was, it went on the poster.

Jacob still had to wear a catheter and a diaper. Almost two weeks had passed, and a nurse came in and encouraged me to do something Nicky and the nurses had been doing; change Jacob's diaper. I had avoided this until now and I gave my reason to the nurse for this.

I told her I wanted to give him his privacy and I didn't feel like I should be the one for the job. She leaned over to me and said, "I get it, but when he goes home, you might be doing this." My heart broke and I was furious at the same time. What? Did she not believe my son could get better? How dare she! Even though I understood her later on, in this moment, I couldn't, but I did what she encouraged me to do. I was humiliated for Jacob, but I knew right then that was what we had to do. Jacob didn't have a shy bone in his body, but this was really pushing it!

On day seventeen, we hit a big one! Jacob was fully awake! He smiled at his friend, Rob, when he asked him if he wanted to go fishing. I still remember what it meant to me to see Jacob's smile again. This was the first day since the accident that we noticed Jacob remembering certain things like his phone and particular songs. I remember how he stared at his phone, looking at it like we do when we see someone familiar, but we can't remember their name or place how we know them. It was like he sort of knew what the phone was, but didn't know how to use it or what to do with it. However, when he heard his favorite songs, I saw a chill version of the Jacob I once knew. It was like he had found something that seemed familiar to him and he didn't seem so far away in his mind. This was the day I felt so thankful because he helped to do regular things like brush his teeth, hold things, and just look around, but only to the left. He was unable to look right and move his head in that direction.

We were introduced to Jacob's physical therapist, occupational therapist, and assigned teacher. I remember how thrilled I was to get the ball rolling and get Jacob started on a schedule. For Nicky and me, this meant so much. It was a step in the direction of starting the road to recovery and getting Jacob back. I was so happy to share this news with the first person who walked through the door!

Later that afternoon, a family member came to see Jacob. I began saying, "Jacob starts PT, OT, and his teacher comes tomorrow!" I will never forget the words this family member spoke to me and the look on his face. He said, "That is the least of your worries." So, what they meant was, *Susan, your life will never be the same; your son is just lying there and can't do anything independently, and you are talking about a teacher coming in to start schoolwork?* This was the total opposite of the response I expected. What I needed and wanted to hear was "that is so great," or anything somewhat encouraging or positive. I could never say something like this or make someone feel this way. I can't relate because, like many people, God gave me the gift of encouragement. I have also learned the importance of putting my hand over my mouth and saying nothing because words can get heated and do more harm than good. I think of the Bible verses in James 3:3-6, "We can make a large horse go wherever we want by means of a small bit in its mouth. And a small rudder makes a huge ship turn wherever the pilot chooses to go, even though the winds are strong. In the same way, the tongue is a small thing that makes grand speeches. But a tiny spark can set a great forest on fire. And among all the parts of the body, the tongue is a flame of fire. It is a whole world of wickedness, corrupting your entire body. It can set your whole life on fire, for it is set on fire by hell itself."[4]

As I thought about how to react to what had been said to me, I said nothing and gave no reaction. I am certain the Holy Spirit put on my heart to stay silent.

I get tickled at myself sometimes when I think of how my mom would react to how grown up I am and how I handle things now.

---

[4] King James Bible (James, 3:3-36) Biblegateway. https://www.biblegateway.com/passage/?search=James%203%3A3-6&version=NLT

I gave her so much grief as a teenager. I rarely ever listened and certainly didn't learn from my mistakes, or if I did, it was done at sloth speed. She would be so proud of how I listen and learn and react in a positive way now instead of going with my impulses and repeating moments that don't turn out the best. I am so glad I chose to ignore an unwanted, hurtful comment on this day, and to not let someone's opinion form a true statement in my mind.

Even though Jacob could not talk, he started following commands. The first day of therapy, the physical therapist came in with a lift and attached this material around Jacob and clasped him in. It looked like he was about to jump out of an airplane. I was still trying to figure out what was going on when my husband walked in. They attached the clasps to the lift and turned the machine on. My heart sank at what I was witnessing. My son was being lifted into a wheelchair. As I turned my face, about to cry, I saw Nicky. He was heartbroken and had come apart. He told them he better not ever see that machine again, and that if anyone needed help lifting Jacob, he would do it. It was unsettling to us seeing our son having to have a machine assist him in this way. Nicky went on to say, "And we also won't be needing this chair much longer because he's going to be walking all over this place."

I am usually embarrassed when my husband gets this way, but this day, I was doing the whoop whoop circling fist motion in my mind. We had to change our perspective and the way we were seeing things in our minds, and think about how we were going to get where we needed to be. I became a drill sergeant.

Chapter Twelve

Where He Has Taken Me

No more lift! He is going to the bathroom! These were such praises, but we still had so many hoops to jump through daily and so many heartbreaking moments to deal with. One of these consisted of our rides in the wheelchair through the hospital. You see, I wanted to create a normal world for Jacob inside the abnormal world we were living in. I wheeled Jacob outside on the deck that was still in the hospital where there were tables and chairs. We were able to get outside and get some fresh air, but the ride to get there was so unpleasant. As I pushed Jacob in his wheelchair, I was constantly wiping his drool and supporting his head so it would not flop to the front and back. As I did all of these things, I drew attention to us and caused heads to turn. I remember how I felt as a mom to see how others stared at Jacob, trying to figure out what must have happened to him. It was a feeling of disbelief and anger, because most people didn't even try to hide it. Some even turned around and continued to watch. It really hurt my heart to see someone look at my son that way. I wanted to say, "How dare you! You are a terrible person! Have some compassion!" This was something I never had to worry about before, and it weighed tremendously on me. So, I tried to retrain my mind to not even make eye contact and just stay focused on Jacob as we went places.

Even though I knew we were going to experience this, I still wheeled my son out daily because I knew in my heart this wasn't Jacob's life. God put Mark 11:24[5] in my heart before I even knew it was a verse in the Bible. Mark 11:24 says, "Therefore I tell you, whatever you ask in prayer, believe that you have received it, and it will be yours." That is exactly how my mom brain and heart worked from day one.

Day twenty-two was "Operation: Get Tebow in the hospital" day. Tebow is our beagle, or basically, our third child. To say we love him is an understatement! The hospital does not allow dogs, of course. The Browders normally aren't rule breakers, but sometimes, we make an exception. If you know anything about Children's Hospital, there are red wagons located at the entrances to let patients use. Lori, Bill, Sally, and Mac loaded up Tebow in a pet carrier and covered it with a blanket, trying to hide what was underneath. All of the nurses pretended not to see what was going on and let us have our moment. It was all top secret until I was interviewed by a news channel and announced it as I was being recorded. As I mentioned to the reporter about "operation Tebow," my husband gave me the throat slitting gesture, reminding me I was not supposed to be telling the state about this. I stopped in my tracks, smiled, and let out a chuckle along with the word "Oops!"

---

[5] King James Bible (Mark 11:24) Biblehub. https://biblehub.com/esv/mark/11-24.htm

On day twenty-three, Jacob
started grabbing his wheelchair
to help get in and out of it.
He also stood with assistance!
Until now, his right arm was
firmly held at around a ninety-
degree angle; now looked more
relaxed. This day was interesting
in physical therapy with his PT,
Mrs. Molly. Mrs. Molly was a
seasoned PT, and she obviously
knew how to get Jacob to do
what she wanted him to do.

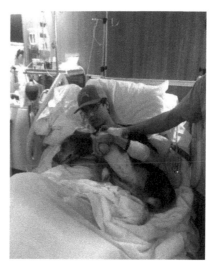

The only way I know to describe Jacob this day was he was in a
mood.

As I walked behind Mrs. Molly, I felt more uneasy because Jacob
had a different look in his eye. He was mad. Mrs. Molly said to
Jacob, "Let's get you out of this chair." She tried talking to him
and coaxing him, but he would not let go of the grip he had on
his chair. Again, Mrs. Molly tried, "Don't you want to get out of
your room? Are you not feeling it today?" Fury started raging in
me because I could see Mrs. Molly was about to give in.

I snapped, "We are not passing up a day of therapy just because
you don't want to comply, Jacob." I told Mrs. Molly, "He's doing
therapy today, and he's getting out of this chair."

Mrs. Molly gave me a look that quickly told me I could shut up or
leave. As I sat and kept my mouth closed, I watched Mrs. Molly
doing what she knew how to do best, which was get stuff done.
She talked with Jacob, saying, "I know you are frustrated and you
must feel angry when your body won't do what your brain wants

it to do. It's okay to be angry." She said, "I will make a deal with you. I'm going to move over to your right side, and if you will look to the right side, you can leave and go back to your room." Nothing happened. Mrs. Molly told him, "I have all day." So, after about forty-five minutes, Jacob stubbornly turned to the right for the first time since his accident and gave her the ugliest look he had in him. She laughed and said, "Thank you, now you can go back to your room."

I quickly saw how much Mrs. Molly accomplished with Jacob on this day. He started using a part of his brain he had not used which was the part that controlled his brain to look to the right. This was a small step in the right direction, but we still had miles to go. My prayers became for Jacob's right side to improve each day, for the drooling to vanish, for him to speak a word, to walk, to get a new occupational therapist that pushed harder, and to pass the swallow test coming up. Swallowing sounds really simple, but when you have a brain injury, your brain doesn't do the simple things it once did, so Jacob had to retrain his brain to swallow again. Jacob was not eating at this time because he had lost the ability to swallow food. He was only getting IV fluids. He was skin and bones. I was not in love with his OT because I felt like she didn't push Jacob, and not much was accomplished. I got my wish!

One weekend, Jacob's OT was not with us and in walked a cute young blonde. I will never forget the day we met Peyton. Jacob's eyes lit up every time we saw her. His OT sessions definitely improved. The change in him was amazing, and what a game changer Peyton was. She had a sweet and stern way of working with Jacob, and the progress they made together was something to witness.

On day 28, I could see a different Jacob. His spirits were up! I felt so proud to be his mom. His work ethic was tremendous. He enjoyed a room full of company on this day, and lots of laughs were heard and grins seen. But on this night, as Jacob, Nicky, and I were alone, my frustrations got the best of me. Living in a hospital this long definitely had the roller coaster effect. I reflected on how many days we had been there and how slow this process was. Then it happened.

I was exercising Jacob's legs as he was lying in his bed. I bent them, straightened them out, and then left his right leg dangling off the side of the bed. I must have been really tired because I had not noticed I had done this until I sat down for a moment and looked in that direction. I reached out and patted Jacob, told him to give me a second, and I would get up and put his leg back on the bed. After resting a minute, I got out of my chair. As I stood up, I saw it out of the corner of my eye. Jacob raised his leg up and placed it on the bed. This probably doesn't seem like much to you, but it was everything to me. It gave me the hope that I needed, and I knew God was hearing me. He heard me when I cried out, when I asked him nicely in prayer, and even when I shouted at him.

Chapter Thirteen

Where He Has Taken Me

I went with Jacob to his swallow test. He was harnessed into a machine where he was instructed to swallow thick fluid and then water, which was much thinner, so it passed much quicker down his throat. We were bummed because he didn't pass the test. He choked on the water as he tried to swallow it. The doctors discussed with Nicky and I that a feeding tube would need to be placed in Jacob's stomach towards the end of the week. Botox injections were started to relax the tightness and tone in Jacob's muscles. Mrs. Molly started Jacob on a walker, and at first, he just stood, but a few days later, that changed. Mrs. Molly's reaction to Jacob's first step is forever etched in my mind and heart. As Jacob's brother, Nick, stood beside him wearing a Ninja Turtle shirt (never understood this), Mrs. Molly moved Jacob's walker forward. Our biggest breakthrough happened next. Jacob picked his left foot up and took his first step. Mrs. Molly smiled the biggest smile we had seen so far as she bent down and danced her way back up! The rest of us were frozen with teary eyes, so thankful for what we were seeing.

On day thirty-two, Jacob went in to have a feeding tube placed in his stomach. As he was having this procedure done, it was very

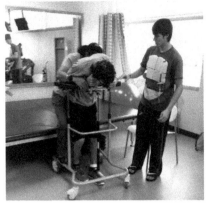

quiet and gave me time to pray and reflect. I reflected on my Jacob and how much I missed his personality, his voice, and his beautiful smile that lit up the bluest eyes I've ever seen. I was so mad at how slow this process was, but I was so grateful to witness it at the same time.

Something I have not mentioned is speech therapy. Probably because Jacob had not shown any progress here. In speech therapy, they worked on swallowing and trying to make sounds again. This was always in my daily prayers but was something that had yet to be answered. Jacob just stared at us in frustration. I wrote in my journal about how scared I was but was always quickly reminded who was in control.

On October 10, 2014, which was day thirty-four, I wrote this in my journal: *I am trusting with a heart of faith that God will heal Jacob. He is able! I am one proud mama to see how motivated Jacob is.*

The next day was a significant one with Mrs. Molly. Mrs. Molly loved to change things up and took us into a long hallway. She asked Jacob a big order that day. She asked him to take fifty steps with a walker. In my mind, I was doubting he would get to fifty steps, but hoped for half of that. As Jacob took his fiftieth step, he didn't stop at there. As he raised his leg again to keep going, Mrs. Molly said, "It looks like we are doing fifty more, Mama." Jacob's football coach caught wind of this and used it with his team to motivate them to always go over and beyond what was asked. He was so proud of what Jacob was doing to get his life back. Things were really starting to look up, and we got our first sound in speech therapy. We got a "ha" with a head nod. But remember, we were on a roller coaster ride; there are ups and downs, and we were about to experience a down.

Day forty-one he was in the worst mood and spirit ever so far. Mrs. Molly came in to take Jacob to physical therapy, and as she reached to help him out of his bed, he did a familiar, firm grip we had seen once before. He held tightly onto his bed. Rage built in me again because, remember, Mama doesn't want him to miss a day of therapy. I went to pulling and trying to force him out of his bed. Mrs. Molly shook her head at me and said, "You are not going to get that boy out of bed like that." I gave up and noticed Jacob staring at something in his room.

His dad had brought his favorite pair of boots and placed them in his hospital room. These were the ugliest, in my opinion, boots Jacob had ever owned. I couldn't believe we paid money for them. His eyes caught them while we were at the World Finals in Texas. We had a break and went boot shopping. Sometimes, Jacob is drawn to clothing and boots that will draw attention to him. Well, these boots certainly did this. They were mostly turquoise with a checkerboard design at the bottom. So, as Mrs. Molly noticed Jacob's attention towards these boots, she asked him, "If you put these boots on, will you get in your wheelchair then?" Jacob gave her a thumb's up. We put the boots on, and Jacob got in the chair. As quickly as he got in, he was out just as fast. Jacob kicked his boots off using the other heel of each of the boots and lunged back toward the bed as he fell in it. Jacob had done exactly what Mrs. Molly had said. He got his boots on and got in his chair, and he was done. She had not stated anywhere in all of this about going to therapy.

So, thinking about this, Mrs. Molly was satisfied and called me out into the hallway. She said, "Jacob is not about to do anything he doesn't want to do today. He is frustrated and he's done. He is mad." He started trying to get up and get out of bed. This was great news, but if we were sleeping and he got out of the bed, he would fall. His balance was terrible at this time, and he had to be assisted with everything. To make the situation worse and Jacob even more annoyed, the nurse brought in a tent bed. So now, he had to be zipped up at night so he couldn't escape.

I read Mark 4:35-41 on this night. I questioned God and asked why He wasn't hearing me. Did He care about what we were all going through? Then, I thought about how Jesus calmed the storm and how the wind and waves obeyed his command. I was so quickly reminded of how much God loved me; He did hear me, and He did care. I also thought about how chill and relaxed Jesus was so many times in the Bible. My reactions were usually not so chill and relaxed when unwanted things happened. But since we have been there, my reactions had started to change from fear to being full of faith.

The next day was the forty second day. I heard Nicky get up before me and unzip Jacob's bed. As I dozed back off, I was quickly startled by the quiet shouting of my name. As I stood up, Nicky said, "Jacob, do you need to go to the restroom?" When we asked this question, we usually got a thumb's up or a thumb's down, but on October 18, 2014, Nicky got a whispered, "Yeah." I lost it and began jumping up and down.

I said, "Can you say Mama?"

Jacob said the quietest and sweetest, "Mama", that I had prayed for forty-two days to hear. Moments later, he looked at me and said,

"Chill." This is the moment I knew everything I had been praying for was right in front of me. I believed it, so I began receiving it! Mark 11:24 smacked me in the face, and it was the best smackdown ever! The best part was seeing the look on his brother's face as they Facetimed and talked to each other.

Chapter Fourteen

Where He Has Taken Me

You had to really listen close because Jacob's speech was very hushed and quiet, but also slurred like when you are listening to a very intoxicated person. So, to others, it might not have sounded like something to shout about, but to us, it certainly was. We asked the nurse to call his speech therapist to let her know. We told everyone, and they all celebrated with us.

The next day, Mrs. Molly came in to have her first conversation with Jacob, and it was so much fun to watch. They both are the kind of people who can dish it out and take it. Mrs. Molly told Nicky and I how much sense the day before made now. He was trying to talk and couldn't, and that frustrated him so much to the point where it worked in his favor. God used that frustration and turned it for good to motivate and push Jacob to speak.

Chapter Fifteen

Wanting My Life Back

I am unable to remember much about the first few weeks in the hospital, but I do remember how I didn't talk for weeks. I had been using thumbs up and thumbs down for everything, and I remember my dad walking up to my hospital bed and asking me if I needed to use the restroom, and I would reply, saying, "Yeah." He yelled for my mom to come and he asked me again. I replied with the same answer. She fell to the floor, crying tears of joy. My parents knew I would be my old self again, even after they were told by doctors that I wouldn't be. They were going to give us the worst news possible in case that was true. Imagine having to relearn how to stand again and having to use a walker to help you. That's what I had to do at the time, and they didn't really see me getting much better, but my parents and I had hope.

I don't remember a lot that happened through the next weeks, but what I do remember is how I felt like I was in slow motion. It was so frustrating not being able to communicate and say what I wanted to. My thoughts and words could not make the connections I wanted them to make. I just remember using thumb's up and thumb's down to communicate the best way I knew how.

My mom always does devotions in the mornings and shares this on social media. She started doing this before my accident. Someone brought us a silver message board. She wrote a different Bible verse on it daily, and faced it so that it was visible to anyone in the room. I woke up each morning and read it in my mind. I remember seeing, "The thief comes only to steal, kill, and destroy. I came that they may have life and have it abundantly." John 10:10. (ESV) [6]

I was still not able to speak at this time, but I thought about all that had been stolen from me. All of the simple things like walk, talk, along with so many others, were gone so quickly, and I felt it would take a lifetime to get them all back. I felt frustrated and at the end of my rope. I wanted to rewind and choose a different path than bull riding. I thought about how abundantly I had lived my life before that night on September 6. I wanted my life back, and I knew how difficult this was going to be. I know my mom and dad, and the look in their eyes was very different. They were sad, mad, grateful, determined, and they put their hope in something bigger than them. Apparently, these were all of the ingredients needed because things started to change for me. I was about to witness two people fight for me and all they wanted for me with everything they had.

I remember lying there one day with the TV to my left, watching and not wanting to look to my right. I wouldn't do it for anything, and my physical therapist came in and turned the TV off, sat on my right side, and said, "When you look over here at me, I'll turn it back on." After a few minutes, I looked over at her with the meanest face and she just smiled at me and said, "Thank you." Everyone was shocked that she fixed the problem that easily. Her name was Mrs. Molly, and she worked with me and got me better faster than anyone would've believed.

---

[6] King James Bible (John, 10:10) Biblehub. https://biblehub.com/john/10-10.htm

Chapter Sixteen

Where He Has Taken Me

The next few days, we noticed Jacob feeling embarrassed. He didn't like an audience and didn't want company. But there were so many improvements being made and at a much faster pace than we were used to. Nick came to visit, and took Jacob to the game room where they played hockey and basketball. In my journal, on day 44, I wrote, "My prayer requests are for the right side to continue to get stronger, for vision to improve, the brain to heal, and speech to improve. My answered prayers are his right arm moved, lots of smiles today, walked on the treadmill, and sat up perfectly." I also wrote, "My thoughts are I am so grateful to God for giving me my son back. God gets all the glory." This was another great day.

The next day, after three attempts, he finally passed the swallow test and he got to eat yogurt! Jacob didn't like yogurt, but today it was like having his favorite food and the best thing he had ever tasted. We had another praise this week during OT. Up until this day, Jacob's right arm had to be casted into a mold that had Velcro that was used to clasp it so he could take it off and on. It started out being casted in around a forty-five-degree angle and then moved up to where it was as straight as he could get it, which was around a one-hundred-degree angle. I can remember many days where I would hear rip in the Velcro where the tone would be too much for Jacob, or he would get sick of it and rip out of it. When the tone kicked in, the muscle tightened up and they wouldn't relax.

The praise I mentioned happened when Jacob was with his OT, Peyton. Peyton was trying to get him to move his right arm and use it more than the forty-five-degree angle, which was the degree he held it as it is firmly tightened into his chest. As they worked on this for a while, our time was almost up when Jacob's right arm moved and straightened all the way out. It was another priceless moment of expressions. Jacob smiled so big as Peyton celebrated. It was a combination of a smile of shock and a Steve Urkel "Did I do that?" It was great.

The next day, we started getting information from Jacob's neurologist about the parts of the brain that had been damaged. We were told with a TBI as severe as Jacob's, Jacob's short-term memory and processing new information will be very difficult.

The next tidbit of information I got was in Jacob's room with a room full of doctors. His rehab doctor, Dr. Davis, announced to me that it was time to go home. We all loved Dr. Davis. I always felt he gave it to us straight with a side of positive. But, as I stood there stunned and terrified, my thoughts took over and I started crying. I went off into a rant. I raised my voice crying. "If you are sending us home, then you are sending me the message that you believe this is as good as Jacob is going to get. This is it!" I was soon guided to a small room where I spoke with two of them. I was completely wrong. These doctors explained how they did keep some patients in Jacob's condition, but went on to say how they had witnessed us taking care of him, staying on top of everything, and basically pushing him too far sometimes. So, they believed the best thing for his recovery was to be at home in a familiar place.

They believed he could make tremendous gains based on what he had done so far; I wept. I was hugged on and cried with at this moment, and it was another reminder of all the people who were for us and cared about this process.

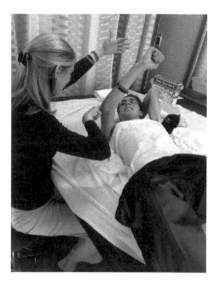

After I gathered myself and all I was feeling, I walked back to Jacob's room. I looked around his hospital room. I gazed at all the photos on the door. I gazed at my positive poster that I updated daily. I took in all we had brought into this temporary room to make it a familiar home for Jacob. I took a moment to myself to relive the whirlwind of the last forty seven days. I thought about how we had witnessed a modern-day miracle. I have read so many miracles in the Bible, and now I had my very own.

★   ★   ★

It was day forty-eighth day at Children's Hospital, and today we got to go home! All of the doctors, Jacob's physical therapist, occupational therapist, and nurses made their rounds, scheduled upcoming visits, and wished us well. His nurse this day came in to give me a crash course in all that was going home with us and encouraged me to do certain tasks all day long until we left in the afternoon. This included all therapies, such as speech, pureeing foods, hooking up and unhooking the feeding tube that he still had, and heavily assisting him in everything. Nicky helped Jacob get dressed in one of his favorite snap button western shirts, Wrangler

jeans, World Final's belt buckle, turquoise checkerboard boots, and rodeo cap. Hours later, we got the discharge paper. I snapped a picture of Nicky and Jacob. It was a picture that captured a crooked smile because of the trauma and a dad who was bending to the side to help his son stand up straight. It wasn't a perfect picture, but it was perfect to me. This moment wrapped up all that is said to be a dad, and how Jacob's dad would always be there to support him.

As we left the hallways I had once prayed so many prayers in, shed so many tears in, and lost so much sleep in, I felt like a scared little girl. I know how to teach and be a mother, but being a nurse was going to be beyond my comfort zone and expertise. I gathered the scared little girl up inside me and thought about all God had equipped me with so far. He reminded me what He is capable of and the "believe you have received it" outlook on life that He had taught me.

We loaded everything up in our Jeep, and we were Demopolis, Alabama bound. We had a two-hour drive home, but it passed by in record time. As we pulled onto Main Street, we noticed a big banner made by friends that read, "Welcome Home, Jacob." We were welcomed by a small crowd of friends, and I arrived home to a clean house. Supper was planned, my favorite wine waited on the buffet for me, along with a spread of snacks. It was such a blessing not to have to worry with tasks like these and just ease into our new routine for the first night at home. Our dog, Tebow, was over the moon to see us all. He ran from one end of the room to the next, bouncing from couch to chair to express how much he missed us.

Chapter Seventeen

Where He Has Taken Me

The next few days of October were a whirlwind. Homebound school services, physical therapy, occupational therapy, speech therapy, and the at home therapy "homework" we were given for each therapy had to be coordinated. I continued to stay at home. Nicky was in and out from his job, and our son, Nick, came for the first full week of being home. We all loaded up in the Jeep to attend Jacob's first physical therapy visit in our hometown at Genesis Rehab. We were really excited to see the plan for Jacob and to watch. We were quickly noticed and given the eye from the owner that said, "Go home, we've got this." As a mom, my heart sank, and I deflated. I wanted to see and be sure Jacob was being pushed and not cut any slack. I am also the "I don't want to miss a thing" mom. But we knew all of the people who worked at Genesis Rehab, as well as the owner, and we trusted them, so we left for an hour and returned on time.

Nick and Mallory joined us on our first outing. We all took Jacob fishing, which was one of his favorite things to do. It was very different this time because it involved packing up a wheelchair. As Nicky put the fishing rod in Jacob's hand, we just all stared at him. We were so happy he was getting to fish. As we watched Jacob, he hesitantly cast the rod. It was like he wanted to start casting, but in the middle, he stopped and backlashed. His coordination was such an issue. He couldn't smoothly do things like casting his rod. It was very frustrating for him, but he handled it as well as could be expected. Jacob had an aggravated look as if he was ready to chuck his rod in the water. Little did I know, there were about to be many days like this ahead of us. Many days of not going smoothly.

November rolled around, and the next few weeks consisted of these therapies and homebound school services along with Jacob's favorite, bow hunting! He went with his granddaddy, Richard. He loves being with his granddaddy because you just never know what events may occur, but today was bittersweet because Jacob shot a deer for the first time since his injury. We continued to want normal for Jacob.

Jacob's football team was still playing, and we were invited to come and pull our Jeep inside the stadium, which was what we did. It was great to see people come up and talk with Jacob. A few weeks later, he was asked to be a captain and his number seven jersey was brought to the house. I remember how I held his jersey close, knowing this would be his last time to ever wear it. We were told in the hospital Jacob would not play contact sports ever again because he would not survive another hit to the head. As the day came for Jacob to be a captain, I soaked up seeing him in his jersey. He was assisted onto the middle of the field by two seniors. The walk took him a while, so his dad met him with his wheelchair. It was a moment wrapped up with smiles and tears because it closed the football door for him.

Homebound school went really well with Mrs. Hathcock. She really boosted Jacob's confidence and was so patient with him. When Jacob did the math problems correctly, he would hear Mrs.

Hathcock say, "Beautiful." So that became their word with each other.

★   ★   ★

As December snuck up on us, I had to return to work. Nick came home to help during his Christmas break in college. As a mom, you realize how hard this was for me to leave men in charge of everyday tasks. I had to get over the idea things would not be done exactly how I wanted them, but what mattered was they got done and Jacob continued to heal. I remember my first day back to work and walking into the middle school building three months later. The first thing I noticed was a sign in the hallway still up. It said, "Praying for Jacob," and was signed by so many students.

The school year crept by and was grueling. "Busy" was given a new meaning. I kept asking the Lord for guidance, protection, healing, and improvements. Seeing God restore, work, and heal before my eyes was nothing short of amazing. I keep asking, seeking, and knocking, just like Matthew 7 talks about. Sometimes, I feel like I'm knocking so hard for so long, but I am not being heard in the timeframe I want. This is when I am reminded to be faithful and continue to trust.

Chapter Eighteen

A Welcome Home

I had an occupational therapist named, Peyton. She treated me using everyday things that I needed to relearn to do like buttoning my shirt, putting on clothes, throwing a football, and anything else that involved me using my hands. She had this hook she made me learn how to use to button my shirts up. It was really difficult and took a long time to accomplish. My least favorite of all the things Peyton made me do was dig countless items out of therapy putty. It was something that looked so easy, but it was one of the most difficult tasks because of how terrible my fine motor skills were.

I loved Peyton. She was one of my favorites and got me to do things the other OT could not get me to do. It might have had something to do with how pretty she was and how big her heart was. I would try anything for her. I couldn't move my right arm, and I remember one day Peyton had me reach for something with my right hand and I did it; I looked at her with a shocked expression. With Peyton, I would learn to gain strength and coordination back in my right arm.

As the weeks went by, it was time to go home. So, on October 25, I left the hospital with a wheelchair and I was walking with a crutch. I arrived home to a small party of people and a huge sign that read, "Welcome Home, Jacob." I went hunting with my dad, brother, and Pop later that day and ended up killing my first deer since the accident. It felt really good to be back in the woods and doing something that I loved, but it was very different from my other hunting experiences. Normally, this would have been something I would have done on my own, but now it was something I had to have assistance with. So even though I was smiling and had a great time, reality set in. It wasn't how I wanted or pictured getting back to hunting, but it was a start. It was a great feeling to get back to something I loved doing with other people who shared my love of hunting. My pop's eyes said it all. He was so happy to see my hunting again.

My parents wanted to get me back to doing normal things that I loved and enjoyed. They knew it was not possible just yet, so Dad asked me to ride to the farm with him. As we drove off, I noticed a smile of satisfaction. Even though we could not yet do things at this time we normally would, like fishing and hunting, it was just the two of us together again in the truck. After riding around and checking on things at the farm, we headed back home. Dad came around on the passenger side of the truck and helped me out. As he shut the door, I think he must have had a lot on his mind because he slammed my right hand in it. As Dad tried to guide me away from the truck, I let out a very whispered, "Ouch." A few seconds passed, and because my reactions were delayed at this time and my mind had to catch up with what my mouth wanted to say, it took me a minute to relay to my dad he had shut my hand in the door! So, as he heard the words "ouch" come out of my mouth and saw the shut truck door with my hand inside it, his eyes became like saucers. He said, "Son, why didn't you say something sooner?" But because of the numbness in my right hand, I hardly felt it.

The next day, I began physical therapy at a rehabilitation center. It was in my hometown of Demopolis. I remember my first day when a therapist said, "It will be okay if you have to use this crutch for the rest of your life." At first, I was in angry mode and really bothered by his statement. I couldn't picture myself at fifteen walking with a crutch, much less for the rest of my life. I said, "Well, I will not be doing that." His words motivated me, and I told him that I wouldn't let that happen. I think he was just trying to motivate me, and I was going to get rid of that thing as fast as I could.

I knew that I was not going to get through this without hard work and without faith in God. There were a lot of days in physical therapy where I would fall trying to relearn to walk again. Leaving rehab one day, I remember my mom saying, "Not many parents get to watch their son learn to walk twice."

Rehab was a long road, and I went three days a week. There were so many things on my list that I needed to learn how to do again, and do it coordinately. We started off small with things like throwing a ball, catching a ball, working on my core, working on side-to-side movements laying down on a mat, walking with balance and coordination, and using the exercise machines. The thing about relearning to do all the things I already knew how to do was they didn't come easy to me. This was very difficult because I was the athletic guy who normally got something the first time I tried. Now, I was learning how to keep at something all day long and get up the next day and try it again. I would continue this cycle for weeks, months, and some things for years, until one day, it clicked, and I finally accomplished what I was working on. It was the most difficult and frustrating time of my life; I wanted to give up, and I tried several times, but I had a mom and dad who wouldn't let me.

They kept me going, and I learned that when things aren't easy, but extremely hard, there is much progress to be made. I learned to look for my blessings here. For example, imagine being a football player, basketball player, tennis player, and anything that involves running, and you no longer have the ability to run. When you do try and run, you look drunk, slow, and uncoordinated. That was me. Even though I don't look drunk anymore when I run, I am still a little slow and uncoordinated, but it is huge progress. Think of something in your life where there is huge progress to be made, and remind yourself things that are difficult to do allow a lot of room to show progress; that progress will bring tremendous blessings.

I returned to school in January, but I was only going half days. Some of my friends were helpful getting me to and from classes. My dad always picked me up at lunch. As time went by, people had their own lives and day to day things to do. I don't think they really knew how to handle the life changes that were going on with me. They didn't know how to deal with their friend suddenly having to live differently. I didn't really feel accepted and popular the way I had before. I got plenty of weird looks or sympathy glances, which is exactly what I hoped I wouldn't get. Many people asked me all kinds of questions, but my favorites were, "Do you remember me?" "What's my name?" These kinds of things were not the problem. Remembering details, recalling things I just did, and learning new material was a tremendous challenge.

I remember one of the first public places we went to was church. I will never forget what Brother Scott, my pastor, said as he saw us. We walked in a few minutes late as the choir was singing. The song was about victory. As we sat down and Brother Scott arrived at the podium, he said, "A victory just walked through the door."

Heads turned and tears were in people's eyes. I also remember the stares. After having a TBI, some people experience ataxia. With ataxia, I showed signs of being drunk, even though I wasn't, and I severely swayed from side to side. I remember how in the church service, I would sit between my parents so when we stood, they could stop me from swaying from left to right.

Chapter Nineteen

Duck Hunting and New Goals

Being not included and not going to parties or gatherings to the extent I was before my accident was hard, but I had more important things I needed to focus on. Everyone else's normal was no longer mine. I went duck hunting in Greenwood, Mississippi with one of my best friends, and we filled our quota on ducks the two days that we were there. We rode a ranger all the way to the blind, so it was easy access. It was a fun and needed trip at the time.

I went to physical therapy the next week, and I was introduced to another physical therapist. Her name was Mrs. Marianne. With

Mrs. Marianne, I would learn to walk unassisted. I worked hard and I took my first steps all alone about a month later. She really got so much out of me and did it in a loving way. She made me feel like I could do anything or achieve any goal I wanted to. Mrs. Marianne was one of my favorite people ever because I could feel how invested she was in my recovery, and she treated me like family. Her spirit was contagious, and I knew instantly she loved me and wanted to get me back to the person I used to be. I worked with Mrs. Marianne for over a year, and she taught me so much more than rehab. She taught me numerous life skills, how to believe in myself, and to never give up. She made me feel big.

I then went to an occupational therapist in Demopolis; her name was Mrs. Beth. With Mrs. Beth, I worked on things that helped with my fine motor skills, like catching and throwing balls, using my fingers to pick up things, and even roping. I never would've thought that I would have to basically start my life over, but I was ready to take on the challenge with the people that I loved, and I knew that they wanted to help me improve. I tried to look at tasks like buttoning clothes as steppingstones, and these little things, which were skills I needed to get back, would lead to bigger things.

I would go home after P.T. and I would walk or run blocks around my neighborhood or go workout in a gym. I wanted to get better as fast as I could, so no one would have to worry about me. I continued occupational and physical therapy for years. I also remember going to the local wellness center and trying to jump rope for the first time. Day after day, I would work so hard to get just one more each time I tried, and it made me excited to see my progression each time I picked the jump rope up. I started videoing myself, and I went from not being able to do a single jump rope to doing thirty almost a year later.

One day, my mom got a phone call from my kindergarten teacher's son, Adam. He was in charge of Upward Basketball, which is an outreach ministry program. I was actually a former Upwards Basketball player, and my dad was my coach. Adam asked my mom if I would speak at the Upwards Basketball banquet and share my story. I put together some Bible verses and what I had gone through. My mom and another one of my teachers put together a PowerPoint with music showing my progress over time. The day came for the banquet, and I was nervous. Several people, a friend of mine, and my family came to listen. Even though I was nervous, this was something that changed my life. Young players came up to me this night, asking to touch my belt buckle, if they could get a picture with me, and I shook many hand.

The best thing out of all of this was to see the look in my parents' eyes. They were proud. Proud of me for taking my story and using all that caused me so much pain and heartbreak and allowing God to use it for His glory. I had heard my mom say over and over again, "Jacob, we have to believe that we have received it; trust God, and have faith, and he will show us His glory through all of this. That is exactly what John 11:40 says,

"Jesus responded, 'Didn't I tell you that you will see God's glory if you believe?'"

God took a person who stumbled and stuttered over his words, who couldn't remember what he wanted to say, who got details mixed up, and He allowed me to share my story with others.

People began to hear about this, and I went on to speak about my bull riding accident at many other churches, programs, school events, and banquets. It felt good to tell my story, to see others make a decision to be a Christian, and to hear how my story helped others. I reminded everyone the importance of never giving up, having a positive attitude. In life, you will probably get something you didn't ask for, so work hard and change your outcome by thinking unreasonable. This made it all worth it and helped me work that much harder to achieve all that I wanted to.

I was told I probably wouldn't drive or do anything "normally." April 23, 2015 was my 16th birthday. This was not anyone's typical sixteenth birthday. The next four months consisted of going to two driving schools as I continued my physical therapy. In July, I passed the test proving the doctors wrong. I'll never forget the first day I drove off in my red truck. My mom followed me out the door like most moms do in this situation. She had her phone in her hand to capture that moment. She somehow must have hit record on the video because I have proof of what happened next. She was doing everything she could to prevent me from driving off. Things like, "Jacob, do you need a water?" "Turn your radio completely off." "These windows are tinted; I don't think you can see. You should roll them down." Even though my mom has her psycho moments, I understood why she felt this way. She just didn't want anything else to happen to me. My mom didn't want to be put back in the same place we had already been. Seeing me come so far was everything to my mom. After my accident, I tried to put myself in my parents' shoes and remind myself how blessed they felt to still have me here with them. When I do this, it helps me see things through their eyes and why they are so protective over me.

Someone told us about a chiropractor team in Mississippi, and we knew they could help me. Dr. Culpepper really made a difference in my recovery. I regained most of my strength and coordination in just a short time working with chiropractors there. I was introduced to a hyperbaric chamber while I was in Mississippi that helped me to get more oxygen. The chamber played an important role in giving my body an opportunity to heal. Getting in the chamber is similar to how you might feel ascending in an airplane or increasing at a high elevation. Basically, your ears have a lot of pressure and they pop.

Later that day, I was told that I was chosen by the Make A Wish program to be given tickets to go to the professional bull riding world finals from Children's Hospital in Birmingham. My favorite bull rider at the time was J.B. Mauney, and he sent me a video telling me that I would get tickets to the PBR, Professional Bull Riders, world finals that year in Las Vegas. This was such an honor for me. I invited my best friend, Justin Kent, on the trip. It was a three day event and it was packed full of things for us all to do. As we arrived at the PBR, a lady greeted us with our VIP passes. We went back to rooms where the bull riders got ready, and we met several of them. J. B. Mauney was late showing up, but another bull rider, Cody Nance, took up a lot of time with me. I showed him some of my rodeo pictures and told him my story. I realized Cody was the kind of person I could look up to. He really had his life together, had an amazing work ethic, and was very humble. After the event, J. B. Mauney met me and I was asked to go backstage where the press conference was held. It was so exciting to be right in the middle of all of the things I normally just get to watch from my living room.

The PBR is in a category of its own. It has top notch riders and an amazing atmosphere. There were so many great rides, and I even saw a rider have a rodeo wreck similar to mine. The only thing that was different about the ride was that he walked away from it with only a concussion and was able to ride the next day. The PBR was the place one day I dreamed of ending up. Even though that dream would never come true, it was amazing to witness a day of a bull rider in the PBR.

Chapter Twenty

Trusting

When I got back home from Vegas, I found out about a guy who was a CrossFit coach in my hometown. I became a member, and he would have me do heavy and hardcore workouts like pulling sleds with tires on them and lots of running. This is where I found out what a burpee was and learned to hate them. I dragged tires, did power clean, ran, and did everything within a time limit. It made me feel competitive again, and the workouts were always different.

When you go through something like I have, you get tired of working so hard and not seeing results quickly. I had already worked my butt off and done everything anyone suggested. My mom and dad were always looking for anything or anyone who had ideas or programs that would help me improve my strength, coordination, and balance. I had hit a plateau, and we had stopped seeing progress, but we always kept trusting. My parents and I always gathered together and prayed before we went to bed. I remember one night of prayer in particular. My mom seemed to be struggling, and she seemed very frustrated. As she was wrapping her prayer up, she ended very differently. It went something like this:

"Lord, I have asked you. I have asked you so many times!" She said these words like she was mad at God, raising her voice at him, frustrated.

As she opened her eyes and we looked at each other, I said to her, "Mom, I think we should do that again." My comments, sometimes, have a way of making light of situations, and we sure needed one at this time. As Mom cried, she began to laugh and then apologized to us and the Lord.

My dad is the hardest of all on me. He is that way because he wants me to be the best I can be. We butt heads daily, but at the end of the day, I always get a clear picture of why he pushes me. It has always been difficult for me to admit when I am wrong or when I mess up. I have always had an issue with this because admitting I am wrong, for me, meant I was a failure. It was hard for me to see my failures as stepping-stones to being able to achieve these things later on.

Sometimes, my family and other people get frustrated with me. I am so used to the phrase, "You aren't listening." It is not that I am not listening. I try really hard and make an effort to remember things I am taught or told to do. Since my injury, remembering things has been the most challenging thing for me. I hear what people say, but then when details are brought up, sometimes I get a look of aggravation because people get frustrated retelling me things that have already been talked about. It is not that I am not listening. It is like what was said to me never recorded in my brain the first time. When I hear it again, sometimes it seems a little familiar, but other times, it doesn't at all. When my parents or other people get frustrated at me, it really weighs on me because I hate to let others down.

I have learned many things through this process, and so many I have been blessed by. But one thing is for sure: things change, and

God moves. One thing I am thankful for now and have prayed so hard for is recalling information and for my memory to improve. God keeps stepping up and answering my prayers.

My eleventh-grade year, I tried to fill my days with all of the things I love. But when you are living a life that is also filled with many different physical therapies, you miss out on things that people my age were doing. I was going in different directions than all of my other friends, and I was pretty much just around my family. People had a hard time, I guess, with all of the changes I had in my life. Having a head injury brings a lot of complications. When you do not have a filter, it can get you in a heap of trouble. At this time, if I thought something, I said it out loud.

I remember attending a local rodeo near my home. As I was walking to find a seat, I recal a young girl who was smoking a cigarette and sitting on the gate. Believe it or not, I used to ride bulls with this girl. She asked me how I was doing, and my response was not the kindest. I said, "I don't talk to trashy women." I think she knew I was kidding, and I really was, but I shouldn't have said it; that's just the way I was at the time. I was very impulsive and said what I was thinking without having a way to filter my thoughts. So that impulsiveness sometimes got me into trouble and made me regret things after the fact. Imagine you have a strainer, and you are trying to strain the spaghetti you cooked. You dump the spaghetti into the strainer and the water goes out, but the spaghetti noodles are caught. I didn't have the strainer I had before so everything I was thinking always poured out. I don't blame people that grew apart from me, but it was difficult. It is hard to describe all of the changes my brain was experiencing. Even though I wanted to filter my thoughts, it wasn't possible for a while, and people looked at me differently. It was a process of relearning how to filter and stop myself from saying or doing everything that was on my mind.

Chapter Twenty-One

Giving Back

Have you ever had something come out of your mouth and regretted it? I believe we have all been there. Anger, fear, or anxiety probably took over in this type of moment. As we all live and learn, hopefully we finally figure out the main ingredient needed to guide us. We need God every day in our lives.

At this rodeo, a young cowboy walked up to me and said, "Are you Jacob Browder?" He had seen my face on social media. When I told him I was, he asked for my autograph. I was a little cracked up, but also it made me proud to see him look up to me.

Through this process, I started listening and stopped talking so much or saying the first things my brain thought of. When I started listening, the Holy Spirit always gave me something to say. Sometimes, my words can be full of wisdom for someone. Sometimes, I speak from experience and give another person a warning of what could come. Sometimes, the Holy Spirit gives me nothing to say. That's when I know to be quiet, just listen to what the other person is saying, or just be there and sit with them. Whatever the situation, if we would just all pray for God to give us something to say, you can bet he will lay it right in the middle of our hearts.

Finishing high school was one of the best things to happen because high school wasn't fun. Walking across to grab my diploma was a defining moment for me. It was the start of something new and a chance to go in a new direction where no one knew me, the mistakes I had made, or what I went through. I had no idea what I wanted to do with my life, but I knew I loved hunting and fishing and spending time in the outdoors. I decided to go to taxidermy school, and I drove to Georgia with my mom. You have probably learned many things about my mom so far in this book. She always thinks the worst. She imagines the worst-case scenario in her mind, and even if it is a one percent chance of happening, she goes there. She insisted she go with me, but thankfully, she agreed to stay in a hotel. Even though I was gone a few weeks, she packed stuff like she was dropping me off for a year.

We arrived at the place where I would study my new skill. Mom seriously thought about canceling and turning around. The place was not at all what she pictured, but I didn't mind it. It was a small mobile home in the absolute middle of nowhere. It was rough, and stuff was scattered everywhere. My mom called my dad immediately and had a fierce conversation about the place he had found. After the shock of the place wore off, my mom pulled in the driveway. Of course, she had to go in, introduce herself, give my instructor food, and sit down and talk. I have learned this process the last few years of my life. It is just going to happen, and I have just accepted it and learned that it is her way.

Learning to mount a deer was not easy. It was difficult, time consuming, and cool. I was extremely proud of my first mount. I went on to another school and got pretty good at it. I was lucky to have learned about things taking time and about progress. This sure came in handy for me here. Mounting a deer is somewhat like doing things over and over again until you get it right, and when you get it right, it is the best feeling. Taking something original, molding it, and bringing it back to life, was something I was now pretty good at. It was really good OT work and helped strengthen my fine motor skills. So much detail goes into mounting, and my hands are really shaky when it comes to using my hands to do tasks that involve delicate details.

After attending another taxidermy school in Tennessee, I was well on my way. My dad and I built a small shop where I was able to work. By word of mouth, I started getting business. After a year of doing this, I realized this skill was a lot of work with little pay. So, I decided to attend a trade school where I got a degree in Machine Tool Technology. This was another mountain I had to climb. All of the material I was learning was not sinking in as quickly for me as for my peers. Learning new material was a process of doing the same thing again and again for it to stick with me. I sometimes got behind other students, but I met some pretty good guys who didn't mind showing me some of the things again when I forgot. This was frustrating for me because I didn't want to stand out. Standing out now wasn't a good thing because it meant there was something different about me. I didn't want to be different. I wanted to be just like I was before and blend in.

I earned my degree in Machine Tool Technology and decided to go for the second part of this degree, which was Computer Numerical Control, or CNC. This part was a little tougher, but things were going fair until COVID-19 reared its ugly head. My classes were moved to online, which made learning this trade more difficult. It is not easy to learn how to use a machine when the machine is no longer in front of you. After four weeks of trying, I dropped my courses.

While I was in college getting my machine tool degree, I got connected with a man my family has always known, Matt Kelley. He is the founder of Equip Ministries, which carries out a productive ministry to eliminate drug abuse. Matt travels to schools, churches, and different kinds of outings to speak to people. He wants to reach schools because most addictions start before the age of eighteen.

Matt asked me to travel with him to different speaking events to help set up and sell merchandise. It was cool to see Matt in action and how he related the outdoors to the gospel and reached people through it. I found it beneficial for me as he related things to hunting and fishing to his messages, because those are a huge part of my life. This tugged at my heart, making me want to get into speaking again. I also got to be a part of hunts that Matt was involved in through Equip Ministries. I met some awesome people who have turned their life around and have been sober because of this program. It has made me see the importance of giving back and helping others who need a break and are having a difficult time with things they are facing. I just recently attended a dinner given by Equip Ministries to wrap up a hunt that donated the deer harvested to feed families. After the dinner, Matt gave his message and shared some success stories. There was a young man sitting at my table. He lost his family through an alcohol addiction. Now, with the help of this ministry, he has been sober for years and is getting his son back. That's big and that's God!

This ministry is close to my heart because, before I was born, my dad was an alcoholic. He was on the verge of losing my mom and my brother, so he made a choice to get help. He went to an in-treatment program and now he has been sober for almost twenty-three years. He has recently had the opportunity to help another person using what he went through. I hate that my dad and family had to go through all that they did, but I couldn't be prouder of my dad. He is the strongest person I know, and he has fought so hard for me to get my life back. I think this is why I fell in love with Equip Ministries, because they helped people like my dad. They give others an opportunity to change their lives and give them a hope for their future. Just like my dad, they have a chance to make a change and to go a different direction in life that equips them for their future. Matt inspires me to find my message as a speaker and use my story to connect with others and equip them with tools they need to get through their challenges and to never give up.

Chapter Twenty-Two

Knowing Who I Am, Now

I have learned so much about life and hard knocks. I have lived through the most difficult of times. Through these times, my mom always said the same thing, which was to just be still. I really never understood what it meant to be still. Now I get it. For me, it meant to put my hands down and to quit going head-to-head with whatever my "bull" at the time was. It meant to walk away and breathe. Being still means exactly that, to be still. It means to find your quiet place and get out of your own head. It means to let go of decision making and the outside voices and to let God be involved.

So here I am, over six years later, realizing God had a different plan for me. What does the future hold for Jacob Browder? I am not doing taxidermy, and I am not using my degree in Machine Tool Technology. I did all of these things without really talking to God about my purpose in life. After listening and trying to do things my way, I have learned to really talk to God like he is sitting right next to me—because he is. I think I have found my purpose in life. I want to return to speaking. I wrote a book about my story that will hopefully inspire others to take life one day at a time, and to never give up, even if it takes you years.

I only dreamed of writing a book. One day, I found myself talking to an author, Ondi Laure from Story Launcher. Meeting her changed my life and made my dream of writing a book come true. We learned how similar we are and how we have gone through some of the same things. I know God had a hand in meeting Ondi and getting my book published, just as God has had a hand in everything I have accomplished. I am running at a pace I am comfortable and proud of. I am doing things in the right order now. I am asking for guidance and I am listening. I am proud to be an author, owner of a landscaping business, and am in the process of getting cattle to raise. Things are not at all what I pictured them to be, they are even better! If God had not allowed me to go through all that I have, He wouldn't have built me into the person I am today. Struggling so much in my life has built me into a much better person. The struggle has taught me so many valuable life lessons that help me through so many things daily. We don't wake up every morning hoping for a great struggle, and that sure wasn't the first thing on my mind on September 6, 2014, but that is exactly what began on this day. It has made me into a person who can tackle anything with time. I have learned that everyone is not always going to be in your life, and people aren't always going to love you through the difficulties in your life; I am okay with that.

All that have I gone through, such as lost relationships with buddies and girls, things I didn't see through, plans that changed, and things that didn't turn out right, are God's plans and redirection to what my purpose is. I pray for the girl I am going to marry, and the friendships God has in store for me. While I am waiting, I am going to continue for God to build me into the right person so I am ready for the girl He made for me and the friendships He will send me. Waiting is something I am well experienced in, and that has given me the time I needed to grasp what was coming. I have had so many dates that, in the end, just didn't work out. It never entered my mind at the time; I was doing it all wrong.

Even though I had a terrible injury in bull riding, it was the coolest and most exciting thing I have ever done, and I wouldn't change doing it. I learned so much from it, and in my recovery that I can use throughout my life. I not only read about miracles, I am one.

God chose me, Jacob Browder, to go through all that I have. He did it for a purpose and to teach my family so many things about Him. He did it to show what He is capable of when the devil comes to steal, kill, and destroy.

My crazy, unreasonable, and fearless mindset I had before my injury has really helped me push through all of my struggles. I have always tried to be determined in my recovery and stretch myself to get my life back. There are days where I feel Satan all over me. He loves to jump in when God is working on me. He loves to get in my head and tell me everything I am not. So, over time, I have learned to redirect my mindset and notice when Satan is creeping in and not let him get the best of me. I know who I am now.

Chapter Twenty-Three

Where He Has Taken Me

Jacob constantly looked to my husband, his brother, and me for reassurance. He wanted to know that we believed he would continue to get better. He asked the same questions at least on a weekly basis. "Can you tell anything is wrong with me?" "How does my walking look?" "How do my eyes look today?" "Do I sound okay?" At first, I couldn't be completely honest. Nicky and Nick were more honest when they answered his questions. Then, Jacob began asking us to videotape him walking, running, and doing other tasks. He could find his weakness and knew we had all not been completely honest with him. This drove him to fine tune things to be the best they could be at that point. What empowered me as his mom was his determination to get his life back and his longing for a sense of normalcy. Seeing my son dig in and find all that he needed to keep going and not give up did something inside me that made me love him even more, if that was possible.

We would make sure we picked our times to talk with Jacob to see how he was coping with all he had going on. Sometimes, all we had for him was just to listen and acknowledge his feelings. It was difficult to have an answer for everything because, most of the time, we just didn't know or have the answers he wanted to hear. Most of the time, the way he responded to adversity amazed us.

Other days, we saw a temper creep up inside him that apparently had been raging, but he kept it all inside until he no longer could. He would always be so apologetic about it all, never wanting to be a burden or add more to our plate.

I remember one of my not so wonderful moments as a mom in February of 2015. Jacob had just started back to school doing half-days. Anyone who knows Jacob knows that he will be wearing a button up shirt, Wrangler jeans, belt buckle, and, of course, boots. At this time, Jacob needed assistance getting dressed. He had some trouble with fine motor skills, so buttons were not his friend. His balance was challenging, so standing and lifting his legs to put on jeans was not much fun for him. I always figured in more time for the morning to assist him. I remember him getting completely dressed in cowboy attire for the day.

As we were about to leave, Jacob said, "I don't want this belt; I want my other one." Changing belts involved not only removing it, but taking off the buckle and putting the one on he wanted. I wish I could say I handled this with grace and quickly changed it. Instead, I raised my voice about how we did not have the time to change it as I snatched it off of him, causing him to lose his balance. I will never forget the look on his face and the way I made him feel. I quickly apologized, and Jacob tried to make me feel a little better. After I dropped him off at school, I went to my school. I made it all the way to the teacher's lounge, where I clocked in, and with other teachers in the room, I lost it and ran to the bathroom. I cried and cried, and I was so ashamed of how I had reacted to my son only wanting to change belts. The shame and guilt absolutely killed me. God sent me two ladies, Jennifer and Trish. They didn't judge me, but looked at me with mom eyes and hugged me. Trish said, "All moms mess up. You have been through so much, and everyone has a breaking point." Jennifer has a way of making light of situations. As she winked at me, Jennifer said, "I guess this was definitely yours." This broke the feeling of shame and of the pain I had caused and brought a smile to my face. They reminded me that I am human. I prayed for forgiveness and prayed for this to be a one-time terrible reaction. I promised myself to always walk away before I reacted.

As July snuck up on us, Jacob got his driver license. I am sure there are moms like me out there who follow their sixteen-year-olds around every time they leave the house, right? Well, I am embarrassed to admit it, but I did. I honestly squeezed him tightly, prayed over him as he pulled out of the driveway, and then ran to get into my Jeep to see for myself he made it there safely. Even though I had a Life three hundred and sixty app that alerted me when Jacob completed a drive and what his top speed was, I had to see for myself he was driving carefully and that he made it there in one piece. Jacob had no idea I was doing this until months later.

Jacob had left for Genesis Rehab one morning, and I did my normal following routine. I knew he was always there at least an hour, so I would go back home and return to the Hardee's parking lot next to the rehab facility to wait on Jacob to pull out. As I was arriving at my normal spot, I saw Jacob walking to his truck a little earlier than normal. I had not made it to Hardees yet! I was at the traffic light in front of Genesis. He was backing out of his parking space at Genesis Rehab, and as he did so, an older lady started backing up into Jacob and he didn't see her. I did what any mom would do, and I beeped my horn as I rolled down my window yelling. I will never forget the look on his face and the embarrassment I caused him. Even though nothing happened to either vehicle, I learned a valuable lesson. When you pray over your child and you say,

"Dear Lord, please give Jacob traveling mercies, cover him in the blood of Jesus, and cover him in your protection," and then you follow your son as he travels just to be sure God is doing what you prayed for, that is the opposite of trusting God with my son. That is me thinking I can do a much better job at protecting him, which is one hundred percent false.

As high school kept rolling, each year went quickly and had its heartbreaking and beautiful moments. These moments were equally there. Jacob asked to be homeschooled, but that wasn't possible. He received some rude comments from kids at school on several occasions and he never told us. I found out about this from another mom at the grocery store. It broke my heart to talk about it with Jacob because of the number of times I learned it happened. Jacob knew he wasn't defined by what others thought of him, but he knew at this time he was not the person he used to be, and he had some physical things that did stick out. He had enough going on, so I really couldn't understand how others could look him in the eye and say some of the things they said. Anger takes over in instances like this, and you get directed to a place you do not want to go. A place where you plot and scheme on how and what you are going to do to that person who hurt your child. What I tried to get Jacob to learn from this was to not allow someone to tell you who you are; you show them who you are. Just because someone gives their opinion and two cents about you, that doesn't make it true.

Jacob passed up prom each year at his school. It was exhausting and tough to watch him miss out on so many things he should be experiencing in high school. It was difficult to attend football games, tennis matches, and high school events that my son should be a part of.

I remember one football game in particular. Even though Jacob was sitting beside me and not on the field, I remember closing my eyes and remembering what he looked like wearing his number seven blue and white uniform. Doing this only gave me a temporary normal feeling again. But what it did after was worse. When I opened my eyes, it reminded me of the present and how he was no longer part of football. I would never see him play again. It's that feeling you get when something that was so much a part of your life no longer is. So, I learned to stop looking back and trying to remember what life was before this happened. Doing this wasn't going to change what happened, and it was only breaking my heart all over again. I discovered the things that happened to Jacob and changed his life; the best medicine wasn't to glance backwards, but to keep moving forward because the glances back kick us every time.

One of the best moments of his senior year was graduation and seeing him in his cap and gown. As we were taking pictures after graduation, Jacob saw Mrs. Hathcock, his homebound teacher. He looked at her on the football field and said their favorite word, "Beautiful." Her eyes filled with tears. My eyes did too, thinking of how many times we all had heard that word in our home.

Leaving Jacob to do things on his own like going to different states to attend taxidermy school, driving to other states to hunt, driving long distances for other reasons, and just doing things on his own was hard for me. I had to trust him to make non-impulsive decisions, to be safe, and for other people on the road not to drive like morons.

Some days, it is so difficult to keep moving on one day at a time and trusting this process. So many times in the Bible, God asks people to keep going even if it looks grim, we are tired, and nothing has happened out of all of the things we have tried. Luke 5:5 reminds

us of that: "'Master,' Simon replied, 'we worked hard all last night and didn't catch a thing. But if you say so, I'll let the nets down again.'" I love the words "if you say so" that are said to Jesus here. This reminds me that when I feel like I am at the end of my rope and I am struggling to hang on, to stop trying to control it all and to give myself grace. So to keep moving on, I continue to remind myself of times in the Bible when others kept going and the reward they received. So, I keep the "if you say so" thought in my mind and keep the faith, trust, and belief I have had the entire time.

I can remember talking with a dear friend of mine during this time about times in our lives where we really struggle. The Bible verse Isaiah 45:7 was the center of it all. We shared many things that have crushed our spirit, but these same things also molded both of us into different and changed individuals. Going through the rough patches has intensified and strengthened our relationship with the Lord. It has grown us! When we realize the

Lord is working for us and He can do a much better job than we can, it gives us PEACE. This is the word I heard my friend speak on this day. She talked about the peace she now has, and I could actually see it in her eyes. It truly brought me to tears!

When we do encounter rough patches, we have an opportunity to see them in a way that can

shape us and change how we handle stressful times. This builds the most important of all relationships. It builds and forms your relationship with the Lord. This is where I realized why the rough patches are important.

Don't you wish we were all given a course in high school or college on the cost of our choices? I know that I should have taken it several times. I have definitely learned the hard way how to keep up my guard and how to recognize when Satan is tempting and stirring around. The phrase "God will never give me more than I can handle" is absolutely false, y'all. I hear this at least weekly. God has given me more than I can handle tons of times in my life. It's the leaning that I do on Him to work in my life and having faith He will be my help that pushes me through times like this.

So how can we see the cost of our choices before we make them? Practice not being impulsive on making decisions, ask ourselves if this is something that we can grow or benefit from, and recognize when Satan is lurking. There are warning signs each and every day where Satan is waiting to hook and reel you in and to cost you everything you love. Don't bite!

Something I have not mentioned yet is the strain this has had on my marriage and family. Yes, we have all stuck together, but there have been days here and there where it wasn't at all pretty. I would sometimes pull out the blame card on my husband on the really tough days. Then there are days you don't pull out the blame card, but you focus your frustrations in other ways.

I remember one day in the grocery store in particular. For months, I continued to pass by the special cheese's aisle because the block of cheese I wanted was over $8. This day, I had had a particularly long and trying day teaching sixth grade and decided to swing by the grocery store and grab the $8 cheese. My rationale was today, I had earned it and I deserved the $8 cheese! I got it, and as soon as I got in the kitchen, I opened it, grabbed a few crackers, and had my moment. Moments later, I wrapped the cheese up and stuffed it in the fridge. The next afternoon, I found myself needing my cheese fix. I opened the refrigerator and smiled to see my husband had perfectly cleaned it out. I thought to myself how sweet it was for him to do this because I know how busy he is too. I searched and searched for the cheese, but it was gone.

My husband and son have named the crazy lady that comes out in me about once a year Nene. As I walked into the living room, I could feel Nene coming to life. I asked, "Where is my cheese?" They both looked at me like they had absolutely no idea what I was talking about. After a little explaining and listening, my husband said, "Something smelled so awful in there, and I threw the cheese out because I thought it was the culprit of the smell." I lost it, and I lost it over an $8 block of cheese. I shouted, "I just opened it! It was $8 and I have been passing it by for months because of how expensive it was and you threw it away?" There was dead silence and a moment for me to gather my thoughts to realize I had just lost my mind over a block of cheese. Have you ever been here? It doesn't feel good after you replay it in your mind, or your husband shows you the footage later because he videotaped the entire scene as it unfolded.

Going to watch our friends' children in sporting events always made my heart heavy, and I sometimes felt like it was punishment. It was difficult just being there as a person, just watching and not as a parent watching their child. I can remember seeing another player wearing the number 7 jersey and how that made me feel. I thought, "That is my son's number 7 jersey!" It saddened me to see someone else in it.

As I sat in the stands, I closed my eyes and found the picture of Jacob in his jersey; for a few moments, I played that in my mind. I blinked and was brought back to all that was truly around me. My son wasn't out there, but he was with me. I didn't feel a part of a lot of things now. None of us did, but Jacob was there with me.

So even though my family had so many ups and downs, we always pulled together for Jacob and kept the Mark 11:24 mindset. I learned to say a lot of "I am so sorry" and "please forgive me" during these years. We all learned what a strong family we had become and remembered this when we needed to. I really think this is one of the key components in our life struggles. You have to allow yourself to grow from your failures and not so great moments, and let it make you better so you can do it better the next time. God has been so faithful to us, and that is what I focus on each day. We all have to remind the ones we love about God's faithfulness in the Bible and here today.

Today, Jacob isn't using his skill of taxidermy or his degree in Machine Tool Technology. We are the proud parents of a son who owns his own "Browder Landscaping," an author, and a future motivational speaker and cattle raiser. He wears numerous hats, and we are so thankful for each of them. I am thrilled God has laid on his heart to start motivational speaking again.

Jacob has taught me much more than I could ever teach him. He has taught me the value of living every day to its fullest and to keep my eyes peeled. There are definitely so many moments which have emphasized the importance of keeping my eyes peeled and taking notice of all that is around me. This is important so that so many things are not taken for granted. Taking to heart things I have learned through heartbreaking experiences and heart overflowing experiences helps me to take it all in every day. It has taught me to live also. Not just live, but LIVE.

Now, when I hear the Tim McGraw song "Live Like You Were Dying," I smile. I smile because of how much sweeter our life is now. I smile because everything we do now has an exclamation point on it. We love bigger, we are kinder people, and we live differently. We live each day like we are dying, and are grateful to see another one.

★   ★   ★

Have you ever looked back at your life and the choices you have made and wished you had done things differently? I am sure we can all raise our hands to that one. It is really easy to see later on and after the fact when you see that damage and chaos around you. But I think decisions and mistakes make us into who we are and can make us better people if we pay attention to the lesson and allow it to grow us. I know when times got tough before Jacob's injury, I would run, shout, and blame. Today, I run somewhere very different. I find myself always running to God, and in prayer, asking for His guidance and direction.

One thing I have always enjoyed doing is walking outdoors. Walking outdoors does so much for me. I can get my daily dose of Vitamin D, needed exercise, and moments to myself. After these last years, I have added something to my walk. I have added talking with God. Talking with God on my walks brings so much into perspective and it makes all that I am feeling much lighter.

I was walking the other day, and I thought of when we were in the hospital with Jacob. We spent some time with other families that were there. Some had never taken their child home. Others left much quicker than we did. Some left without their child. We were exposed to so many different families, each having their own walk with God. During this, it made me see how big God really is. He not only hears me thanking Him, asking Him for help, and also hearing me have "words" with Him, but He's walking with so many others at the same time. He really is like our best friend. God has walked through it all with me.

My family is now very much aware of Traumatic Brain injuries and has been tremendously impacted. We find ourselves researching and following others who have been impacted to see if we can learn anything new or help others. It helps and gives us all hope to know how others get through their challenges as a family and to see how their lives moved on in a positive way.

I have looked at the date, September 6, as the worst day of our lives for years now. Watching my child have to relearn again everything he already knew how to do was tough for me. It was heartbreaking to see him continually knocked down and faced with everything being much harder now. I know his pain was much more.

Now, over 6 years have passed; I look at it differently. We have changed so much. When I look back at pictures, videos, and remember all that Jacob has gone through, I see how God brought us through each year and how he restored and still is restoring Jacob. My Mark 11:24 mindset got me through it all! "Therefore, I tell you, whatever you ask for in prayer, believe that you have received it, and it will be yours." So that's what we do. When we pray, we believe we've already received it. Whatever you are hoping to receive today, I encourage you to take the Mark 11:24 mindset. Write in on sticky notes, put it in picture frames, and repeat it over and over when days are tough. Be the cheerleader and the over-the-top mom someone needs. Turn the no's in life to possibilities that are eventually achieved. Look at your pain differently and move your feet. Don't look at your "bull" as too big of a giant for you, and remember, little successes create big accomplishments.

When life doesn't go as you plan, it is important to have or establish a strong foundation of faith or your life will be destroyed. You will be left with your life all in pieces and not know how to get through it all. You see, when life doesn't go like we planned, we have the opportunity to make it even better than we planned it all out in our minds. I am so blessed to have Jacob with me. Life did not go as we planned for Jacob, and it has been the hardest thing to walk through. God has taken us through every bit of it. Even though my life has not gone like I planned, my eyes have witnessed, and are still witnessing, more than I could ever hope to. The Lord has moved all in the right time for us.

The Lord's plans allowed my family a second chance. I got to see my son walk, talk, and do all the first things a child does all over again. I got to see God restore my son piece by piece. I am still seeing the Lord answer my prayers today. So, you see, when life doesn't go like we planned, make it even better. Keep telling God that you need Him. Keep asking and don't let the pressures of life make you give up. I end every day now counting my blessings, and I know how absolutely blessed I am!

Proverbs 24:16 says, "For the righteous falls seven times and rises again, but the wicked stumble in times of calamity."[7]

New Year's Eve is a time for us all to look back at the lessons that we learned, the blessings that came, and a time to reflect on our yesterdays. My New Year's Eve happens much more often because

---

[7] King James Bible (Probers, 24–16) Biblehub.https://biblehub.com/esv/proverbs/24-16.htm

I look back a lot to see where we started. I have looked back at the things I learned through my failures. I asked myself many questions, but the one that sticks out to me is, "How can I use my yesterdays?" Can I use them to do things differently where I failed? This is so difficult because we have to be honest with ourselves and learn the truth about ourselves; for me, most of the time, it isn't pretty.

So how can we build on our failures? I certainly do not have all of the answers to this question, but one thing I do know is we have to get back up no matter what. Jesus is our biggest cheerleader, and he wants us to get back up every single time. Every time I decided to get back up and build on what I learned, I was that much closer to knowing I could succeed if I just stayed the course and asked for guidance and perseverance. Let's pray that we do a few things differently and get closer to winning the battles we are all in.

"My flesh and my heart may fail, but God is the strength of my heart and my portion forever," Psalm 73:26. [8]

I heard Clemson's football coach, Dabo Swinney, say how he was blessed to have a "front row seat" to witness things. When talking about his team, he said, "I can relate to these words. I feel so honored to have a front row seat during Jacob's restoration and trusting the process."

"Trust in the Lord with all your heart, and do not lean on your own understanding. In all your ways acknowledge him, and he will make straight your paths." Proverbs 3:5-6 [9]

---

[8] King James Bible (Palm 73:26) Biblegateway. https://www.biblegateway.com/passage/?search=Proverbs%203%3A5-6&version=ESV Psalm 73:26

[9] King James Bible (Proverbs3;5-7) Biblegateway. https://www.biblegateway.com/passage/?search=Proverbs%203%3A5-6&version=ESV

Applying Proverbs 3:5-6 to our daily lives reminded us to not to depend on what we were seeing in the "now" and to trust the path that would lead Jacob to the ending we prayed for, total restoration. I made Jacob a promise a long time ago. I promised him I wouldn't stop pushing him until he could do the things he wanted to again, and I promised him I would never stop praying for complete healing. God prepared us for the tough journey, and we have remained faithful in trusting him. Very few people have had a "front row seat" to God restoring Jacob. The ones that have, have seen him from the beginning to now, and they have witnessed a miracle.

So that deep sense of responsibility I mentioned earlier really drove me to use up each moment of every day. It helped me remain focused on what we faced daily and how to tackle and jump over hurdles. It reminded me of all that I hoped for Jacob, and what he wanted in life was there; we just had to keep reaching for God's hand and praying for unreasonable goals to be accomplished. I seek the Lord every morning and find all that I need throughout the day from Him.

Chapter Twenty-Four

Where He Has Taken Me

Beginning to get over our past "MAJOR" mistakes can be a season in life of feeling defeated. Sometimes, the feeling of being defeated can last for longer than we want. There is one mistake in my life that replays in my mind nonstop. Moments where I rewind the ripple effects and try to stop them and change the decision that I made that day. Forgiving myself has been the hardest thing because of what it cost someone else. As Jacob's mom, I felt I failed him. I failed him, and knowing that is heavy.

But what I have learned, or what the Lord has opened my eyes up to is to look for the good. I can promise you it is there. Mistakes can really grow a person up very fast if you choose to learn from them and let them make you into a wiser person. Really LET IT CHANGE YOU. I have forgiven myself for signing a waiver that day at the rodeo school where Jacob was injured.

Something so significant through it all is how the Lord has equipped my family. It is easier to recognize this as we get older. Whatever I have gone through in life, I have always made it through because God provided me all the strength I needed. I wasn't wise enough to see it until now because I had never taken the time to really think about how I get through the toughest of times. Now I have taken the time to visually see looking back into my past and have noticed He has been there all along. Unquestionably, Jacob's journey has strengthened my prayer life. Going through something so tremendous, and praying yourself and others through it, is the pivotal and powerful moment.

To anyone who is facing and living this out right now, my heart hurts for you. I encourage you today to find peace in your situation and forgive yourself, or you will always feel like a failure and so defeated. Through countless prayers, I found forgiveness and was able to finally forgive myself for not protecting Jacob.

Whatever road you are walking down in life and you wonder where God is, remember He's already there. I often listen to the song mentioned earlier in this book, "I'm Already There." As I have learned more about the Lord, this is exactly how I feel. Whenever the unwanted hits, "HE's already there." Whenever I feel like the walls are closing in on me and the hits keep coming, "HE's already there." When HE doesn't answer my prayers, while I'm waiting and continuing to pray, "HE's already there."

So, I will close on this part of our story for now with reminding all of the readers of the gifts God has given me through this process of healing and restoring Jacob. He has given me a hope and expectation of things to happen if you trust in Him. He has given me my proudest moments as a mom. He has taught me to react differently in unwanted circumstances and to not face them with fear, but with a heart of faith. I am forever grateful for the things my eyes have seen. For all of us, God's handiwork is evident through each and every day. Witnessing this amazes me and makes my heart so full. Healing, sunsets, babies, mountains top views, and the ocean are just a speck of God's beauty. I'm such a blessed and thankful mama for the things my eyes have seen.

What does the future hold for Susan Browder? I hope to spend tons of time with my grandchildren and cherish their moments of growing up. I hope to watch Jacob flourish as a young man and for this book to open so many doors for him as a motivational speaker. I hope to get an opportunity to speak at events and possibly write another book. I don't know what is in store for me, but I am amazed and blessed by the path and ride God has taken my family on.

A former pastor of mine, Brother Grant Parker, had something he said to me and others every single time we left his presence. He would say, "Keep your hand in Jesus' hand and your eyes on the cross." This is a quote that I think of almost every day because it makes me think of how keeping my eyes on Jesus through it all has built a trust in the Lord that no one can take away from me.

I will never forget where we started on the road to recovery with Jacob. It was like looking at a hallway in the hospital and not being able to see the end. I use all of my experiences and the knowledge I have gained to guide me in my life today. My experiences have grown me spiritually, and none of them have been squandered. All of them are used for a purpose now.

I have also learned the way I respond to the moments and difficult days makes a dramatic difference. There have been many days I thought we wouldn't make it. Building the kind of faith I have now keeps me going and reminds me not to worry and stress myself out. I know God has equipped me. I know I have a more productive life today because of the experiences we all went through. These experiences felt impossible at the time, but it is so cool to see how God has used these things to guide me. God calls us to serve others and Him with our talents He has given us. I am not good at a great number of things, but I am well versed in using good or bad experiences to guide me. I feel like God has gifted me in this to help others who are going through life and looking down the hallway, not being able to see the end. By the way, the end of the hallway looks a lot like this. In Jesus Name We Ride.

Chapter Twenty-Five

The Bull Didn't Win

I just had my check up at Children's Hospital in January of 2021. My rehab doctor, Dr. Davis said I have made remarkable progress. I have spent the last 7 months going back and forth to Birmingham to do physical therapy at Vulcan Performance and Rehab. My PT is Sean, and he has done some amazing things with me. He only started with focusing on my right side, which is my weak side that I lost use of. Targeting my right side has caused me to do things more symmetrical and coordinated because it has strengthened what was so weak and allowed my right side to catch up with my left. As I walked through the office door to see Dr. Davis, I was ready to show him the results that Sean had given me to show him. Dr. Davis said, "I don't need to see them." It is very evident!

Hearing from others and their comments on how great I look means the world to me. I hear it from my parents all the time, but sometimes, I feel like they just have to say it. Hearing it from a medical professional or other non-family members really fills me up and makes me proud of where I am.

Don't you love all of the hiccups and snags of life? Just when I feel like I have clawed my way to the top of something I have been fighting for, "bam!" My feet get knocked right from under me. Now, I am back at zero!

Awhile back, something like this would have thrown me into a pit of panic, and I would have lacked an important thing called faith. I do not even attempt to comprehend how God works all of my failures, problems, and bad choices out. I just know He is able, and He does. God roots for us to push past our hiccups and snags of life and for us to be persistent during the journey. Whatever your journey is right now, don't let your persistence and determination be off duty. When you keep at it, you will see a glorious unfolding because your story has only begun.

So, what motivated me to write a book with my mom? I honestly just wanted to tell my story. I wanted to show people out there to overcome all that life throws at you; you have to take the bull by the horns daily. I battle something every single day, and you do too. Life is going to give us all the difficult parts sometimes, and that is just a fact. Mine has been difficult much longer than I wanted it to be. I never thought it would take me over 6 years to get back my life, but it has. Heck, I'm still working on getting all of me back. But I get up every day with a never give up attitude, and I promise myself to never stop having the mindset that I have.

Whatever you are facing today, make a plan, and make sure God is dead center. Some days will certainly be more challenging but regroup and refocus and think about what you want in life; don't let anything stop you from getting all out of life that you hope for. Hope is what got me to where I am today.

So, you see, the bull didn't win. I did. What was meant for evil, God intended for good. Whatever your "bull" is in life, don't let it win. Never stop praying for what you want in life, even if it takes years. Don't ever take anyone's "this is as good as it's going to get," or, "this is all the healing you are going to do." I love to witness God's work and receive His blessings. It may take longer than you thought, you may get really tired, but don't give up on anything or anyone. I am in awe of how my life has changed. I have witnessed so many miracles, and I believe I will see Him do it again. I can testify to His goodness. God reminds me daily of four words. The bull didn't win.

Acknowledgments

Since 2014, Jacob and I always start our thank-yous to the people who have always had our backs. Thank you, Lord! We are so grateful to many doctors, nurses, physical therapists, occupational therapists, family, friends, and rodeo. A special thank you to an overly dedicated husband and father, Nicky. Without you, we would both be lost. Thank you, Nick, for being your brother's keeper. Thank you to all who have been the hands and feet of Jesus. It took a great deal of praying to get us to where we are today.

CPSIA information can be obtained
at www.ICGtesting.com
Printed in the USA
BVHW051709220721
612646BV00022B/1171